Beginning SharePoint Communication Sites

Understanding and Managing Modern SharePoint Online

Second Edition

Charles David Waghmare

Apress®

Beginning SharePoint Communication Sites: Understanding and Managing Modern SharePoint Online

Charles David Waghmare
Mumbai, Maharashtra, India

ISBN-13 (pbk): 978-1-4842-8959-4   ISBN-13 (electronic): 978-1-4842-8960-0
https://doi.org/10.1007/978-1-4842-8960-0

Managing Director, Apress Media LLC: Welmoed Spahr
Acquisitions Editor: Smriti Srivastava
Development Editor: Laura Berendson
Coordinating Editor: Mark Powers
Copy Editor: Kezia Endsley

Cover designed by eStudioCalamar

Cover image by Steve Johnson on Unsplash (www.unsplash.com)

Distributed to the book trade worldwide by Apress Media, LLC, 1 New York Plaza, New York, NY 10004, U.S.A. Phone 1-800-SPRINGER, fax (201) 348-4505, e-mail orders-ny@springer-sbm.com, or visit www.springeronline.com. Apress Media, LLC is a California LLC and the sole member (owner) is Springer Science + Business Media Finance Inc (SSBM Finance Inc). SSBM Finance Inc is a **Delaware** corporation.

For information on translations, please e-mail booktranslations@springernature.com; for reprint, paperback, or audio rights, please e-mail bookpermissions@springernature.com.

Apress titles may be purchased in bulk for academic, corporate, or promotional use. eBook versions and licenses are also available for most titles. For more information, reference our Print and eBook Bulk Sales web page at http://www.apress.com/bulk-sales.

Any source code or other supplementary material referenced by the author in this book is available to readers on GitHub (https://github.com/Apress). For more detailed information, please visit http://www.apress.com/source-code.

Printed on acid-free paper

"The Lord is my shepherd; I shall not want."

—Psalm 23:1

First, I would like to say thanks to Almighty Lord Jesus Christ for offering me yet another opportunity to write this book. I owe everything to Him. I take this opportunity to praise and glorify Him for all the wonderful things that He does for all. God Bless.

I would like to dedicate my book to the following:

My dearest parents—my father, Mr. David Genu Waghmare, and my mother, Mrs. Kamala Waghmare—who laid the foundation of my career. Without them I am nothing. I thank God for my best Mom and Dad.

My adorable wife, Mrs. Priya Waghmare, for her love, encouragement, and care.

Table of Contents

About the Author

Charles David Waghmare is working with one of the biggest Oil and Gas corporation of the world since 2019 as a business analyst in the area of Microsoft 365. He previously worked for Capgemini for eight years in various roles, including as a Yammer community manager, a manager of Drupal-based Enterprise Knowledge Management systems, and a developer of a Knowledge Management platform for a Digital Customer Experience (DCX) organization using SharePoint Online. He managed client references and knowledge assets related to Artificial Intelligence and customer experiences (CX) and promoted Microsoft Azure chatbots to automate processes, as well as developed proactive conversations with users and created new use cases.

Before Capgemini, Charles worked with ATOS (Erstwhile SIEMENS Information Systems Ltd.) for a period of five years. During his tenure, he was a community manager of SAP-based communities at ATOS, where he managed communities using TechnoWeb 2.0 (a Yammer-like platform) and on-premises SharePoint. Charles was also a global rollout manager for a structured document-management system built in on-premises SharePoint.

Charles loves reading motivational books and his favorite book is *The Monk Who Sold His Ferrari*. He is currently pursuing an executive MBA degree from the SP Jain School of Global Management (Graduation: March 2023).

Contact Charles through email at `charles.waghmare@gmail.com`.

About the Technical Reviewer

Kapil Bansal is a lead DevOps engineer at S&P Global Market Intelligence, India. He has more than 14 years of experience in the IT industry, having worked on Azure cloud computing (PaaS, IaaS, and SaaS), Azure Stack, DevSecOps, Kubernetes, Terraform, Microsoft 365, SharePoint, release management, application lifecycle management (ALM), Information Technology Infrastructure Library (ITIL), and Six Sigma. He has worked with companies such as IBM India Pvt Ltd, HCL Technologies, NIIT Technologies, Encore Capital Group, and Xavient Software Solutions, Noida, and has served multiple clients based in the United States, the UK, and Africa, including T-Mobile, World Bank Group, H&M, WBMI, Encore Capital, and Bharti Airtel (India and Africa).

Acknowledgments

Alwin Fernandis, my beloved friend who is not with us anymore, But his memories are eternal.

Sridhar "Sri" Maheswar, Supply Chain consultant, NNIT, my beloved friend, for his support.

Pravin Thorat, BU head at ATOS, for his prayers and good wishes.

Cohort members from my executive MBA batch (Middle East 03) and **faculty members** at the SP Jain School of Global Management.

My Church, The Salvation Army, Matunga Corps.

Introduction

A Microsoft 365 SharePoint communication site is a great place to share information and interact with other users. It can also be used to create portals, department-specific sites, and projects that are specific to your company. With the ability to create multiple types of websites, you can easily reach a wide audience.

Through SharePoint communication sites, you can experience seamless experiences working with Microsoft 365 services such as Forms, PowerApps, Power Automate, Yammer, Teams, OneDrive, and others. If you are searching for a tool to manage your content, documents, and information, SharePoint communication sites is a great option.

What Is In this Book

Through this book, you will learn how to create visually appealing communication sites so your organization can manage information easily and effectively. You will also be able to improve the ways that you communicate and collaborate with coworkers.

You can efficiently store and manage information with the help of a centralized repository of your company's data. SharePoint communication sites also allow you to automate various processes using other Microsoft 365 services.

The Audience

This book aims to help individuals and organizations devise content management strategies in order to improve their organization's performance. It also aims to help employees connect with information and develop new opportunities. In addition to helping improve the efficiency of their organizations, this book aims at helping Gen Y employees create a new experience and contribute to their organizations' digital transformation journeys.

CHAPTER 1

An Introduction: SharePoint Online Communication Sites

Charles David Waghmare [a*]

[a] Mumbai, Maharashtra, India

Introducing SharePoint Online Modern Experience

The modern version of Microsoft's popular content management system, known as Microsoft SharePoint Online Modern Experience, is designed to be more performant and compelling. It makes it easy for anyone to create beautiful and mobile-ready sites. With Modern Experience, you can build visually appealing experiences using the SharePoint Online sites called *communication* sites and *team* sites. SharePoint sites referred in this book are part of SharePoint Online service available in Microsoft 365 (M365) product.

The classic style of building websites in SharePoint is done using a hierarchical structure that includes subsites and collections. This type of architecture can be very hard and time-consuming to maintain once it's built. With SharePoint Online Modern Experience, every site is a collection that's associated with a hub.

© Charles David Waghmare 2023

C. D. Waghmare, *Beginning SharePoint Communication Sites*,
https://doi.org/10.1007/978-1-4842-8960-0_1

1

The most effective websites and applications help visitors navigate quickly and easily to the information they need. They also help users solve problems and make informed decisions. The principles and practices of page navigation and site design are applicable to modern and classic versions of the platform.

Although the principles and practices of page navigation are applicable to both versions of the platform, there are different options that you can use to implement navigation. For instance, while the classic navigation experiences are still very useful, they are not as widely used in modern versions. The hub site concept is more widely used in SharePoint Online Modern Experience.

In the past, when it came to designing a site with a classic platform, you had to customize the various elements of the design to match your organization's brand. Unfortunately, this method can be very time-consuming and can make the experience inconsistent on different devices. With Modern Experience, you can easily customize the various elements of a site to match your organization's brand. This method can be applied to a group of sites or to all of your organization's sites. If you're planning on implementing a publishing site or a publishing-enabled site in your organization, you're probably aware of the importance of creating attractive and performant pages that can easily be accessed by a large number of people. With the help of modern communication sites, you can easily create pages that are mobile-ready.

One of the most important factors that a website designer should consider when it comes to search is the ability to find information quickly and easily. A new Microsoft Search feature exists in SharePoint Online Modern Experience. A box is placed at the top of the page, in the header bar. Microsoft Search in Modern Experience is different from other search engines because it is contextual and personal. It shows results differently, even when you type the same words the same way. It also shows different results depending on where you are in the world. For instance, if you're searching for the root of your tenant in Microsoft Office, you might see different results depending on where you are in the world. The new Microsoft Search feature in Modern Experience provides users with a variety of ways to find what they need, including searching from a hub or a group of sites. This search can also find content from a list or a library.

Modern Experience is designed to provide a more performant and compelling user experience. This is done using various factors, such as the speed at which pages are rendered in the browser and the perceived end-user latency.

A classic Microsoft site can be created with a feature called *variations* to allow it to support multiple languages, as shown in Figure 1-1. Sites created with Modern Experience take advantage of this feature and make the content in their intranets available in various languages. The user interface elements of the site can be shown in the language that the user prefers. You can also translate and provide news posts and pages from other communication sites to your preferred language. One of the main differences between the modern and classic versions of Microsoft's site is that the former allows you to create a separate subsite for each language. The latter, on the other hand, allows you to create a corresponding page within the same site, but with a language-specific folder.

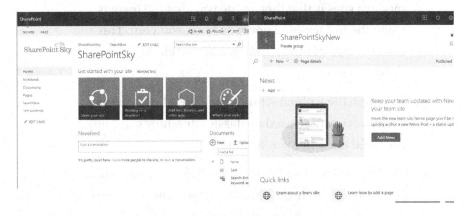

Figure 1-1. *A glimpse of the SharePoint classic and modern experiences*

This section covers the pros of modern sites, and how they make information more compelling. It also covers how Microsoft sees the future of its platform and how it can help developers build applications.

The pros:

- Modern sites are the future of SharePoint, so they're the way to go for anyone who wants to use SharePoint. This means that if you're planning on using the latest version of the platform, modern sites are the way to go.

- Modern sites reflect the way that Microsoft is trying to modernize its interfaces and its platform. Previous versions of the platform didn't support various devices. This eliminates the weeks and months needed to make sure that your sites worked seamlessly across different devices.

- Modern sites are significantly faster than their traditional counterparts. In some cases, they can improve performance by up to 50 percent. One of the main factors contributing to the success of these modern sites is that they're the way that the team is using the framework known as Microsoft.com. This is a new type of model that focuses on client-side development.

- Although the webparts built using the Microsoft.com framework can be used in classic sites, they can't be accessed the other way around.

- The latest versions of the Microsoft.com framework can be used on mobile devices. The goal of modern sites is to look great regardless of the browser you use.

- Most of the applications that use the Microsoft.com framework, such as Microsoft Teams and Groups, automatically provide modern sites. This means that if you're planning on using classic sites for your intranet, modern sites are the way to go.

Although there are many advantages to choosing modern sites, there are still some disadvantages that you should consider when it comes to building a site. One of these is the lack of a site/subsite structure. This is because modern sites are created as collections. They do not include features, such as security inheritance, that are typically built into sites.

The cons:

- One of the biggest issues that clients have with the modern search is the lack of features such as results sources and refiners. Although Microsoft is developing a way to push search results through the Graph, it is not yet feasible.

- Modern sites are limited in their ability to change the interface. For instance, they can only add a light theme on top. Classic sites, on the other hand, have the client's timeline and budget as their only limitations.

- The lack of site provisioning is also a major issue that modern sites currently lack. It is not yet known when this issue will be resolved.

- The lack of a consistent modern site experience is also a major issue. For instance, the home page might look like it is modern, but the next page might look like it is a classic site.

Not every product is perfect, and with the kind of investments being placed into SharePoint Online Modern Experience, it is evident that these cons will be addressed.

SharePoint Online Features

Up to this point, we have talked about SharePoint Online and its power to facilitate content management and collaboration. This section covers the features that make this possible and that create rich user experiences. These features are very easy to use.

File storage: Provides options to upload, store, and share files.

External sharing: Share files with your suppliers, partners, and clients outside your organization.

Content management: Manage and organize content such as Web Content Management (WCM)—Intranet, news, articles, and posts—with metadata, records management, and a retention policy.

Team sites: A dedicated place for your team to collaborate and share documents, news, and information.

Communication sites: Broadly communicate your message across your organization by publishing beautiful content and keep users informed and engaged in topics, events, and projects.

Intranets: Share your customer stories, leadership reviews, new customer wins, organization charts, and what is happening in your organization.

Mobile apps: Access your content anywhere at any time using mobile apps.

Automate work: You can automate processes with alerts and workflows.

Discovery: Discover valuable content and people when you need to.

Search: Search and you will find what you want.

E-Discovery: Discover content in electronic format for legal and audit purposes.

Data Loss Prevention Capabilities (DLP): Use advanced DLP capabilities to monitor data loss and information security protection.

In-place hold: Prevent content from being edited or deleted.

Note   These are the standard images used to denote these SharePoint features.

Microsoft is continuously endeavoring to add new features to the SharePoint communication site to build compelling experiences for their users and developers. These features are based on feedback provided by end users and beta testing from their customers and users.

The old look of the Microsoft Teams in its previous versions was upgraded to an ultra-modern one in 2019. The new version includes a variety of new features and functions, such as a news publishing engine that eliminates the need for a dedicated chat group. This eliminates the need for integration between various platforms. One of the biggest changes are the improved communication sites. These sites are designed to allow users to share information related to their business with their group. There are three communication site templates in the new version: Showcase, Blank, and Topic.

Here are some of the new features of communication sites with Modern Experience:

- List and libraries: Microsoft went a step further in developing Microsoft 365, which is a robust version of its software that allows users to keep all their important information at their fingertips. The new features of the app include a modern list and libraries that allow users to easily access all of their data. There are also handy tabs that allow users to copy and move data. In addition, the app has a new feature that allows users to filter their data using conditional formatting. This method allows them to share their information with their desired users without exposing the full data.

- Modern home page: The new and modern version of Microsoft's website, known as the SharePoint home, is a sight to behold. It features a sleek and modern design that allows users to store all their important information from their various communication sites and teams. This new feature also brings together all the activities that you can do on these sites in one place.

- SharePoint framework support: This feature is not a new addition, but an improvisation of the old framework support. In the latest version of SharePoint framework, Microsoft introduced a new framework that allows developers to create webparts that can be used on both the online and offline versions of the site. This is very useful for developers who want to create multiple webhooks for working on list items.

- Change to OneDrive: On-premises users can now sync their files and folders with OneDrive using Windows 10. This is facilitated using Next Generation Sync Client. This new feature is the latest improvement to the way users can work with various innovations in the app.

- Changes to the App Launcher: The new App Launcher also brings a more modern look to the way users interact with the Windows 10 platform. It allows users to easily transition between their online and on-premises environments.

- Integration with Power BI and Power Automate: There is seamless integration between Power Automate and SharePoint Online to automate processes using SharePoint communication sites. Power BI facilitates publishing reports to any communication site page.

Although the new features in the app are impressive, there are still some features that were not included in the current version of communication sites:

- Digest authentication

- Code-based sandbox solutions

- Multi-tenancy

- Incoming email automatic mode

- PowerPivot gallery and refresh

- Visio services and Silverlight-based rendering

- SharePoint business intelligence scenarios

Differences Among Communications, Teams, and Hub Sites

Exploring SharePoint Hub Sites

Before you learn about the details of the various types of sites that can be created on the platform, you'll first take a look at the internal sites available on the platform. These are divided into three main categories: a hub site that connects people, a team site that enables collaboration, and a communication site that broadcasts information. This communication site is a collection system that can be used to manage your content. See Figure 1-2.

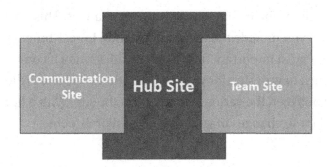

Figure 1-2. *Different SharePoint online sites*

Communication sites can be hub sites, but not necessarily team sites. This section explores the various benefits of creating a hub site and discusses this concept in more detail.

A hub site is an organizational intranet building block that brings together various elements of an organization's website. It's also referred to as the connective tissue of an organization's communications and team sites. The key principle of these social and digital intranets is that each section is designed as its own collection.

A hub site can be used to manage a variety of aspects of an organization's website, such as its communication and team sites. It can also be used to keep track of the latest information about the organization. Most commonly, a hub site is created from a content management system such as Microsoft SharePoint Online.

Previously, multiple subsites were used to bring various elements of an organization's website together in one place. These designs were not very flexible, and they required users to navigate through the site collection's shared navigation. Due to the nature of the design, certain features, such as classification and retention, were required for every site. This means that you must regularly enable these features for all collections.

Regardless of whether you want it or not, change is inevitable in your business. Successful organizations are well-equipped to handle it, and they can increase their value by adapting to it. The content on an organization's intranet changes as the business environment changes. This is why it's important that you provide the latest information in real-time.

One of the most important factors to consider when it comes to implementing a new design for your organization's website is the relationship between the various elements on the site. With a hub site, you can easily adapt to changes in your business environment.

Differences Among the Hub, Communication, and Team Sites

Table 1-1 explains the differences among the hub, communication, and team sites.

Examples of Hub Sites

A team site is a collaboration site that aims to create a unified experience for its users. A communication site is a news or information site that aims to connect other sites. A hub site, on the other hand, is a combination of these two types of sites and it aims to create a unified end user experience. With a hub site, you get a combined experience of communication and team sites.

IT Department

The IT department is composed of various teams that work together to create amazing user experiences. These divisions include application management, database management, server maintenance, cloud services, software installation, quality, and communication. These teams are responsible for keeping the applications running smoothly.

It is very difficult to understand the complexity of an application's operation due to the number of steps involved in maintaining and restoring it. For instance, if an application is down, the users might not be able to connect to the appropriate IT team to resolve the issue. A hub site for IT helps users navigate through the various branches of the organization and find the most up-to-date information about the issue (see Figure 1-3).

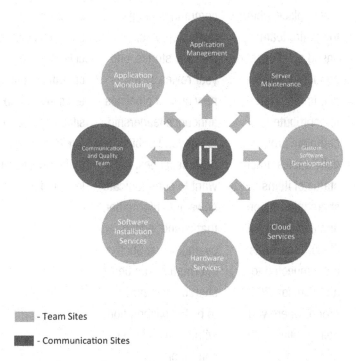

▓ - Team Sites

■ - Communication Sites

Figure 1-3. *Hub site of an IT department*

Figure 1-3 shows a typical IT department hub site. It's a communication site that connects various team sites and enables end users to access information from the group. This is done through a process known as *connectivity*.

Table 1-1. *Comparing Hub, Communication, and Team Sites*

	Team Site	Communication Site	Hub Site
Purpose	**Collaborate**	**Communicate**	**Connect**
Scenario	You want to create a workplace where the entire team is based at an onshore/offshore location and is required to contribute to complete project deliverables, tract status of items tasks, share information, and exchange new ideas. Team sites are connected to an Microsoft 365 group, where you utilize collaborative tools such as Microsoft teams to make collaboration possible.	You want to communicate new customer wins, success stories, end year reviews, and new project pipelines; announce leadership teams; and publish CEO messages. You want to communicate news and information that cannot edited by end users. Such information can be shared on Yammer to build collaboration within the end user community.	Creates a combined experience for end users by connecting collections of communication and team sites. Hub sites organize these families of sites to maintain a common look and feel.
Content Authors	All members are content authors who jointly create and edit content.	Dedicated group of content authors and large group of readers or content consumers.	Authors of the team or communication site who have configured these sites as hub sites.

(*continued*)

Table 1-1. (*continued*)

	Team Site	Communication Site	Hub Site
Governance	Defined by the team involved in the collaboration.	Defined at the organizational level to ensure the correct communicate goes in the relevant messages.	Defined by the owner of the team or communication site who has configured them as hub sites.
Created By	Site owner	Site owner	Global admin or SharePoint admin in Microsoft 365
Examples	1. Team site created to collaborate on day-to-day business challenges, propose solutions, and improve customer satisfaction. 2. To create user engagement during campaigns. 3. To respond to customer RFPs.	1. Communication site created to communicate annual leadership reviews. 2. Communicate annual company results and performance. 3. Share information about company events.	Hub site could exist for various departments, such as HR, IT, and other business units.

Human Resources (HR) Department

Human resources is a collection of departments that include various areas such as talent acquisition, recruitment, and compensation. Having a hub site that connects all these departments helps ensure that new employees can find the resources they need.

A buddy is usually assigned to new employees to help them navigate the various resources available on the human resources hub site. However, if the information on the site is updated, there is no need for a buddy.

Figure 1-4 shows an HR hub site that's also a team site. It connects various team sites, such as recruitment and talent acquisition, to communication sites, such as payroll and compensation.

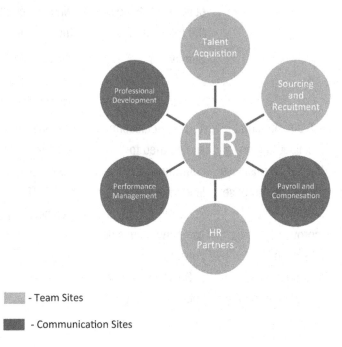

- Team Sites

- Communication Sites

Figure 1-4. *Hub site of HR department*

Exploring Communication Sites

After looking at the differences between communication sites and hub sites, it's time to explore SharePoint communication sites independently. A SharePoint Online communication site is a place to share information, such as news, reports, statuses, and events, in a visually captivating format with a large audience that's part of your organization.

SharePoint communication sites are ideal for internal collaboration during internal campaigns, news and insights, business highlights, year-end leaders review, and new customer wins. To jumpstart user collaboration, communication sites provide configurable templates. These templates make your life easier when communicating messages to large audiences in a short amount of time.

Communication sites are accessible across various devices. Users can consume information using mobile devices available through SharePoint apps. They are easy to access, engage with, and create content from any device. SharePoint communication sites are awesome ways to share information and collaborate in your organization. Creating SharePoint sites has become a very simple process, with out-of-box features and zero coding needed. Communication sites transform your current communication channels and improve your end users' experiences.

You can create a beautiful communication site in seconds using the SharePoint home available in Microsoft 365. Then you can improve your methods of communicating and collaborating with large audiences, integrate your existing collaboration channels into a SharePoint communication site, and plenty more. Communication sites allow people to create and share periodic updates beyond email.

Creating SharePoint Communication Sites

Here are the steps for creating SharePoint communication sites. These steps are simple and easy to understand:

1. Sign in to Microsoft 365.

2. From the App Launcher available on the top left of any Microsoft 365 service (or access www.portal.office.com), select the SharePoint tile. At the top of the SharePoint home page, you will see the Create Site button and then the Create Communication Site option, as shown in Figures 1-5 and 1-6.

17

Figure 1-5. *Option to create a site*

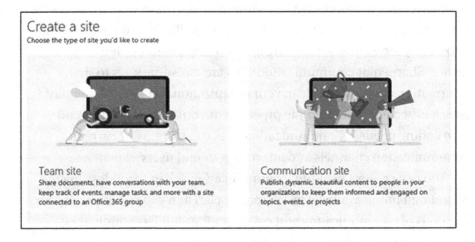

Figure 1-6. *Choose a team or communication site*

3. Select one of the following site designs (see Figure 1-7):

   – Topic, to share information such as news, events, and other content.

   – Showcase, to use photos or images to showcase a product, team, or event.

   – Blank, to create your own design.

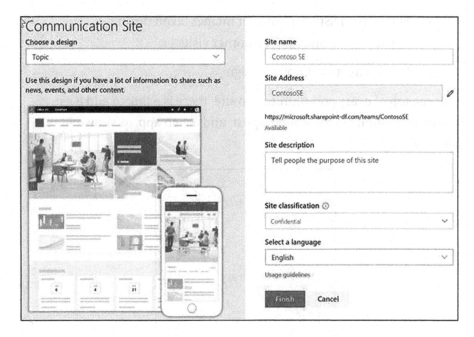

Figure 1-7. *Choose a site design*

4. Finally, update the site name, site classification, and language as needed. Then click Finish to create your communication site.

What Do Communication Sites Include?

You can create a blank communication site from SharePoint Online and use the following design options, which come with a set of default webparts to design your communication site. You can add, remove, or reorder webparts whenever you want. Here are three design options:

- Topic: Publish information such as news, events, and announcements

- Showcase: Display photos or images taken during events, conferences, or customer visits

- Blank: Create your own design

At the top of every communication site, there is a link to add a list, a Document Library, a page, a new post, and a web app, as shown in Figure 1-8.

Figure 1-8. *You can add a new list, Document Library, page, news post, or web app to your communication site*

Let's now look in detail at the different options available to design sites. When you select an option (Topic, Showcase, or Blank), you see several webparts available to design the site:

- **Topic**—Under Topic, you have the Hero, News, Events, and Highlighted Content webparts.

  - **Hero**—Generates focus and visual interest on your page. A maximum of five items can be added to a Hero webpart. You can also add images. The Hero webpart is included by default in all communication sites. Once you click the Hero webpart, it appears prepopulated with images, text, and links and you can modify them or add your own. This webpart has a tiled layout with five tiles and you can modify them from one to five (see Figure 1-9).

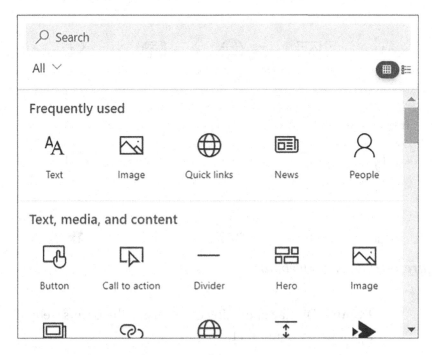

Figure 1-9. *An example Hero webpart*

    – **News**—You can keep your team in the loop and continue to engage with them with successful stories using the News webpart. Using this webpart, you can create eye-catching posts like new customer wins, company-wide announcements, and project status updates with enriched graphical information. See Figure 1-10.

Figure 1-10. *A News webpart*

– **Events**—Display upcoming events using the Events webpart, as shown in Figure 1-11.

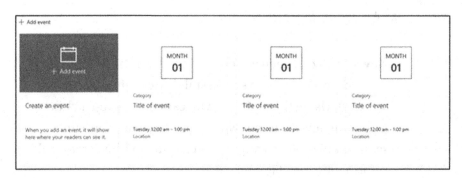

Figure 1-11. *An Events webpart*

- **Highlighted Content**—This webpart displays content from the Document Library or from certain sites to highlight content relevance. You can use this feature to highlight your company employee policy document or code of conduct, for example.

- **Showcase**—The Showcase design option is available in communicate sites, and it has its own set of default webparts.

- **Image Gallery**—To share a variety of images.

- **Blank**—When you start with a blank communication site, there is no need to remove webparts that you do not need. You just choose your page layout and add the webparts you want.

Note   The images shown in this section are demo images and do not link to a production SharePoint site. They are simply used to describe the communication site features.

One of the main components of Microsoft's content management platform is its web-based content management system, known as *SharePoint Site*. It is a collection of libraries, apps, and pages that can be used to create and manage various types of websites. The most popular of these are the team site, hub site, and communication site.

Exploring Communications Sites

A communication site is a great way to share a story with your team members, clients, and external collaborators. It allows you to highlight achievements, goals, and milestones without giving away any rights to the audience. On the other hand, team sites have fewer content authors. This means that users can keep up with the changes and events happening on the site.

With a simple and effective design, your communication site can become more efficient and effortless. One of the most effective ways to summarize a communication site is by displaying updates and news in a visual format that grabs the attention of the readers. Also, you can let your users know about the various services and products that you offer.

A communication site is a part of a hub site. The various elements and features of this site distinguish it from a hub and team site. A communication site's navigation pages are designed to guide the reader through the various content sections. They also provide content snippets and header buttons. The destination page is the point where users can find the content they're looking for. It should include a search bar so that users can easily find content. A showcase-type communication site is ideal if you're planning on displaying videos or images of your team or products.

A lot of features and functions can be found on a single platform, such as document management, security, and asset libraries. Employees can get all the information they need at their fingertips, so they can complete their tasks faster and more efficiently.

With the ability to integrate other Microsoft tools and business systems, such as Microsoft 365, you can easily create a customized version of SharePoint for your company. It can be used to improve the efficiency of your organization.

With the ability to connect and communicate with multiple people working on the same project, SharePoint can help keep everyone up to date with the latest developments. Its robust Document Library makes it easy for team members to store, manage, and search their knowledge assets.

You can also target content based on an individual's location, department, or seniority. This method helps employees get the most relevant and useful content.

One of the most important factors that businesses consider when it comes to choosing a content management system is the flexibility of its platform, such as Microsoft's SharePoint Online. The platform allows users to create and manage content efficiently. Aside from managing content, the platform also helps boost productivity by allowing users to collaborate and automate their processes.

The platform acts as a central hub for all your content management needs. It features a variety of tools and features that allow users to create and manage content efficiently. Its integration with Microsoft's Office services also helps boost productivity. Consider these features:

- Hubs or repositories

- Easy collaboration

- Seamless integration with Microsoft 365 services

- Creation of custom solutions

- Extensive OneDrive storage based on subscription

- Enhance information security and governance

Most companies want to know the various ways that they can use Microsoft's platform to improve their processes. Here are a few examples of how easy it is for companies to customize the platform and automate their processes:

- Intranets

- Document management system

- Knowledge management

- Process automation

- Creation of flows

Before you start using Microsoft 365 or the SharePoint platform, it is important that you understand all the ways that it can help you improve your business processes. This book gives you a good understanding of the various features and benefits of this platform. The use cases and benefits of the platform also help you understand how it can help you automate your processes.

Creating SharePoint Online Communication Sites

A communication site is a type of website that allows people to share information with a broad audience. It typically only has a few members who contribute content to the site, and it's not ideal if you're planning on working with other individuals on a project. A team site, on the other hand, is a better choice if you're interested in working with other people on a project. It allows all the members of the team to contribute content, and it also limits the information that can be posted to a specific group.

Here are the steps to create a SharePoint communication sites:

1. To sign into Microsoft 365, go to the top-left corner of the page and choose the App Launcher icon for Office. In the top-left corner, you can also select the SharePoint tile. If you don't see the tile, click the Sites or All button if you want to keep it.

2. On the home page of Microsoft 365, click the + Create site button shown in Figure 1-12 and choose the communication site option. In the box that appears, you can give the new site a name and add some text that describes its purpose.

Figure 1-12. *Create Site option for communication site*

3. In the Site classification section shown in
   Figure 1-13, you can choose the type of information
   that will be stored on your site. The options are
   related to the lifecycle and sensitivity of the
   information that will be stored on your site.

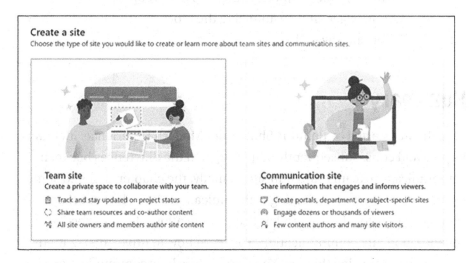

Figure 1-13. *Configuration of communication sites*

4. Name your communication site and, in the box that
   follows, add some text that explains its purpose. If
   enabled by your admin, you can also choose a site
   classification that fits your needs. There are various
   options that can be used to describe the information

that your site collects, such as sensitivity or the lifecycle of information. Finally, choose a language that you want to use for your site.

5. After you finish creating your site, it will automatically appear as one of the sites that you're following. It will not inherit the navigation or permission settings of other sites. You can share your site with other people by clicking Share a Site.

6. After you create a communication site, you can start to customize it using webparts, customizing the SharePoint template, using the Hero webpart, adding pages, and customizing the Modern Experience overall.

Summary

This chapter started by defining SharePoint Modern Experience, including its pros and cons. Subsequently, it investigated the differences between communication, teams, and hub sites. Finally, the chapter explored some use cases and discussed creating communication sites. The next chapter shows you how to adopt SharePoint communication sites for effective collaboration and communication. You learn how to drive organization-wide campaigns using this site. You also explore how communication sites help you communicate and collaborate with the end user community in an efficient manner in order to create a community environment.

CHAPTER 2

Effectively Communicating and Collaborating Using SharePoint Communication Sites

In the previous chapter, you gained an overview of SharePoint communication sites with Modern Experience and learned about hub and teams sites. This chapter covers different implementation techniques to effectively communicate and collaborate SharePoint communication sites in different business scenarios. It also provides different techniques to create user awareness, launch campaigns for engagement, and create intelligent and informed communities. This chapter primarily focuses on the following topics:

- Creating user awareness for communication and collaboration

© Charles David Waghmare 2023
C. D. Waghmare, *Beginning SharePoint Communication Sites*,
https://doi.org/10.1007/978-1-4842-8960-0_2

- Creating a plan for implementation to roll out new use cases

- Executing campaigns using communication sites

- Using SharePoint communication sites for leadership communications

- Measuring the success of adoption

Keeping this focus in mind, you will learn to effectively communicate and collaborate using SharePoint communication sites. Further, you will get experience in how communication sites are used when collaborating and communicating with users, customers, and suppliers, learn to build user guidelines, launch campaigns around communication sites and, finally, develop ideas to increase leadership adoption for communication sites. Let's start by discussing creating user awareness.

Create User Awareness for Effective Communication and Collaboration Using Communication Sites

User awareness is one of the more important aspects when it comes to deploying new products or services in your organization, as it's important that people are well informed about the products they are using or will use shortly. By adopting the user awareness approach, organizations build a friendly relationship with the user community, in order to get feedback, suggestions, and input about its products. There are various approaches to creating user awareness and you can rely on communication sites to build awareness.

When you talk about user awareness of a product, this means you try to communicate the product's details, features, benefits, and business value and provide hands-on experiences to the user community. When we meet a new person, we might be uncomfortable talking to them without an introduction; however, when they are introduced to us by an acquaintance, we tend to get an idea about them and adjust our communications accordingly. User awareness works along the same lines; if you can introduce your products, your user community will be more likely to accept them. This does not mean that everybody will accept them, but user awareness is a good approach to make products well accepted by the user community.

Here are some techniques for rolling out communication sites, through the process of engagements:

- Beta testing

- Super user or champions communities

- Leadership announcements

- Critic communities

- Success stories

Beta Testing

Beta testing is often adopted by Software as a Services (SaaS) products during their rollout. During beta testing, product owners give select users in the community an opportunity to test new features or functionalities available in the production environment. This technique offers various benefits in terms of user awareness, such as:

- Understanding new features to be launched

- Testing their workings

- Figuring out their side effects

- Getting hands-on experience

- Reporting bugs inside a feature or functionality

- Discussing the business benefits with product owners

- Reducing the chances of failure

- Releasing better-quality features due to feedback from the user community

- Increasing user satisfaction

- Getting buy-in from the user community

- Building a good relationship for future releases

Beta testing is therefore a technique through which one makes users familiar with products and new features by directly involving the end user community that will be directly impacted.

Microsoft communications sites have been actively performing beta testing on its Microsoft 365 products. To make communications sites more user friendly, the organizations must involve their users in beta tests. Those users often help the organization during rollout or launch by becoming a super user or champion.

Communication Sites to the Super User or Champions Community

The super user effectiveness implementation aims to upskill, connect, and engage the super user community in order to help the end user community be more effective. This section shows that getting the super user (SU) community to adopt and implement communication sites results in acceptance of these communication sites by the end user community.

The main objectives to set up a super user (SU) community are:

- Super users become engaged in their role and act like owners in their community

- Leadership becomes committed (and is seen to be committed) to the super user community

- End users are aware of the communication site features and rollout process

- End users are aware of the changes that will impact them

This super user community approach is designed to provide the structure required to achieve the communication sites' rollout objectives. The approach confirms the key stakeholders involved in the rollout, the SU community, and the main communications channels available during the rollout phase. It then provides detailed audience journeys and detailed key engagement activities needed to take stakeholders from awareness to commitment to ownership.

To get a sense of how a super user community contributes to a product rollout, the organizational structure shown in Figure 2-1 is a super user community. It will collaborate and connect with different groups in order to enable a successful rollout.

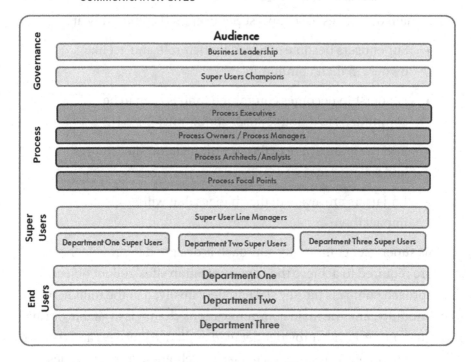

Figure 2-1. *Super user audience during rollout*

Figure 2-1 shows a four-layered organization, which is generally part of any organization during the product rollout. process These four layers are governance, process, super users, and the end user community. Let's look at the role of each layer during the product rollout process.

Governance:

- The business are the owners of the super user community

- Engagement with business leaders is carried out by the super user community

- Super users from the business leadership side take a key governance role regarding implementation and link the implementation process to the business

Process:

- Due to the process-specific nature of super users, process owners also have a responsibility/interest in super user performance

- There is a requirement from the project's perspective to include process owners, process managers, and process architects/analysts in the super user community

- Process owners will be engaged and aligned with the business stabilization workstreams

Super Users (SU):

- Super users and their line managers are engaged by the super user champions

- Part-time super users and full-time super users require different types of communication

- Super users are the focal point of the implementation communications

End Users:

- End Users are made aware of the changes affecting them

Let's now look at the key communications channels that are used during the super user effectiveness product rollout process. The SU Effectiveness Team aligns with the business workstream and uses their channels of communication when engaging process leaders.

- **Support website**: Hints and tips, training, "find your super user," and so on.

- **SharePoint communication sites**: Status/KT/Wiki/ information sharing in the SU forum. One-stop self-service shop for all super user-related content. Expert directory to support the community.

- **Mailers**: Standard format (header/text style, sender, etc.). Super user champions send these to the end user and super user communities.

- **Webcasts**: Core messages and ways of working. Presenter-led format for key groups on the SU implementation. Two-way communication is available.

- **Virtual meetings**: Status/KT/information sharing in an PFP forum. Ad hoc meetings with key business representatives. Two-way communication available

The following list of activities ensures that you effectively utilize your super users during product rollout. Let's start with on-boarding activities for the SU community:

- Welcome new super users to the community

- Engage existing super users

- Introduce super user champions to super users

- Introduce and explain support tools and processes

- Provide updated SU roles and responsibilities and SU profiles

- Explain the know-how about the product

- Provide clarity on the training approach

- Re-launch the super user community

- Explain the super user succession process

Create Super User Engagement:

- Create a webcast approach

- Review and agree on the approach with SU champions and the process support manager

- Develop and agree on material with the SU champions

- Arrange training sessions

- Invite interested attendees who want to be future SUs

- Conduct sessions

- Follow up

Participation Limits for Super User:

- All super users

- SU business champions (to front)

- Process focal points and process support manager
  (to front and support)

- Super user effectiveness team (to front and support)

- SU support first level support – L1 (to assist)

Before going through the super user journey, let's review the super user initiative discussed so far. We started with a four-layer organization, where super users can work with other layers of the organization in order to create effective standards to communicate and collaborate using communication sites. Then, you saw key communications channels used during product rollout, and finally, you saw a list of activities to be performed that will ensure that you are effectively using super users in the product rollout process.

In order to become a super user, you go through various steps such as aware, understand, collaborate, commit, and own. Becoming an SU is systematic progression and includes adopting products, as shown in Figure 2-2. Buy-in from super users is very important during product rollout, as they stand behind process managers during implementation by answering end user queries, giving them ideas for adopting products, and creating new use cases.

Microsoft communication sites need advocates like super users so that they are accepted well into the organization.

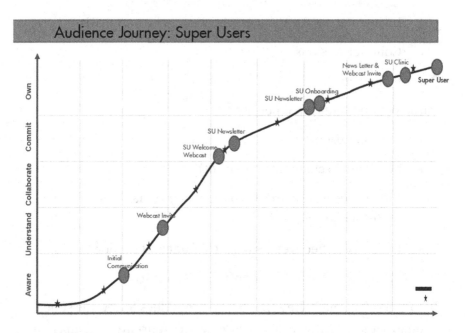

Figure 2-2. *Super user journey*

Leadership Announcement

In my experience as a Yammer rollout manager during my tenure at a Global French IT company, two kinds of rollout processes are common. Top to bottom rollout (i.e. driven by management) and bottom to top rollout (i.e. indirectly driven by management). The user community will judge the quality of the product regardless. My Yammer rollout was bottom to top and I had to evangelize the good message of Yammer to the entire company, build a pool of super users for assistance, and build Microsoft relationships. This role was challenging, not in terms of roles and responsibilities, but in terms of sustaining Yammer as an enterprise collaboration platform. On a yearly basis, leadership would recommend a replacement for Yammer and I had to do my best to make an argument for keeping it.

The Yammer platform included engagement, but very few in leadership remained active on it. In fact, many users asked during training sessions whether leadership was using Yammer and for what purpose. To get better leadership engagement, we rolled out the following Yammer events for the leadership teams:

- YamChats –Online question and answer sessions on Yammer with leadership teams.

- Leadership events for Yammer: Whenever there were business leadership events, we included a small session on Yammer.

- Built content to educate leaders covering the following points:

  - On Monday, start a new conversation.

  - On Tuesday, reply to an existing conversation.

  - On Wednesday, like one message.

  - On Thursday, invite a colleague to join Yammer.

  - On Friday, follow one new Yammer user

- Conducted Yammer webcasts with leadership teams.

- Published Yammer success stories from leaders.

- Convinced the leadership team to be part of the super users program.

- Our Group Chief Technology Officer was Yammer fan,
  so we leveraged his connection to promote Yammer to
  the leadership teams.

- Leadership teams are often on the road, so we
  launched a campaign for leaders to download the
  Yammer mobile app and win goodies.

- Organized Yammer so that leadership teams could talk
  about their Yammer journeys.

Such leadership engagement helped the user community see the value
in adopting the program. From a general end user perspective, if leaders
are not using a product, the product does not seem to have business value.
Lack of leadership engagement is a big challenge when you are performing
a bottom to top rollout. Eventually, you will have minimal support for your
product. Gaining support from Yammer super users improves the Yammer
adoption rate.

The main objective behind narrating this experience is so that you can
replicate this experience during the Microsoft communication sites rollout
process. Here is a list of things that you need to be aware of during rollout:

- Identify whether the rollout model is bottom to top or
  top to bottom

- If it's bottom to top, create a plan to build the super
  user community and identify top leaders who support
  communication sites.

- Regularly engage with the super user community and
  leadership teams that support communication sites.

- Build content for leaders such as this:

  - On Monday, contribute to a Topic.

- On Tuesday, share a Topic Card on Yammer or Teams.

- On Wednesday, Share a People Card on Yammer or Teams.

- On Thursday, contribute to knowledge centers with your experience.

- On Friday, share a couple of knowledge center pages with wider communities.

- Conduct a communication sites webcast about adoption with the leadership team.

- Publish success stories from leaders.

- Convince leadership team to be part of the super users program.

- Leverage leadership connections to promote communication sites in the leadership teams.

- Organize a Microsoft communication sites leadership lunch to talk about their experiences.

- Conduct a whitepaper competition on how you can effectively use Microsoft communication sites.

- Conduct online question and answer sessions with the leadership team on Microsoft communication sites related topics.

Unless and until there is leadership buy-in, the end user community will not take the rollout seriously. An email from a top leader such as the CEO supporting product rollout makes an immense difference because the user community then understands the business value of the product. Therefore, it is important that you involve leadership teams in order to effectively collaborate and communicate on SharePoint communication sites.

The Critic Community

As opposed to the super user community, it is also good to have a critic community during the rollout phase. A critic community is designed to support product rollout, but in a different way. It provides continuous feedback and scope for improvements. The objective of this community is to review new product features and functionalities, user engagement, super user engagement, leadership engagement, and other aspects, in the form of feedback and scope for improvement. Why do you need a critic community? The benefits of pinpointing early signs of failure and risk enable you to act proactively. Here are some advantages of having a critic community:

- Provide early indication of failure or risk during the rollout phase.

- Get a different perspective of the products from people wearing different hats to provide continuous feedback and scope for improvement.

- Act proactively to mitigate risks and fix issues.

- Challenge super users in their day-to-day promotion of the product.

- Make leadership teams part of the critic community to understand why they are uncomfortable using products.

- Develop pain areas that prevent user engagement.

- Make the product stable and highly interactive.

- Eventually makes the objectives of the product rollout
  clearer and more transparent.

A critic community will help you make the rollout objectives very
transparent, create scope for improvement, and help create better content
for users to access platforms and create user engagement.

Success Stories

We have come to last technique of creating user awareness, which is the
success story. These are stories or business scenarios in which users
benefitted from using Microsoft communication sites. It is quite common
that unless and until users hear something good about the product,
they do not take it seriously. Whenever you hear something good about
a product during rollout or any other phase, it becomes an eye-opener.
Therefore, during the rollout phase, it is of utmost importance to share
success stories. They will improve user engagement and membership,
and create business value for the products. Success stories are also an
important aid to renew product contracts and make product owners aware
of business value. The success story template in Figure 2-3 captures the
success story of Microsoft communication sites, which is shared with the
user community to promote engagement.

Username	
Business Division	
Issue	
How Communication sites resolved issue?	
Efforts saved or money saved	

Figure 2-3. *Success story template*

The next section looks at one strategy and approach to running a
Microsoft communication site campaign.

Microsoft Communication Sites Campaign Overview: Strategy and Approach

In this section, you are going learn about the strategy and approach of
Microsoft communication sites campaign. The name of this campaign
is the Microsoft Communication Sites Literacy Campaign. This section
covers a campaign overview, campaign definition and goals, good
communication sites, bad project communication sites, the scope of the
communication sites campaign, and several other topics. Let's start with
Data Literacy campaign overview.

Data Literacy Campaign Overview

This section covers the what, why, how, who, and when aspects of the
campaign, as shown in Figure 2-4.

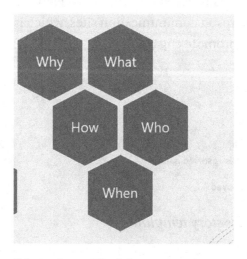

Figure 2-4. *Four Ws and one H of the campaign*

- **What**: Campaign will increase user awareness, achieving business excellence using communication sites across the organization.

- **Why**: To support operational excellence, make sense of the repositories, and create accessible, trusted data. This is done through tacit and explicit knowledge of the organization's systems, people, and employees and understanding how to use data and where it came from.

- **How**: A global, centrally coordinated but locally executed program across business/functions, leveraging different teams (a top to bottom rollout).

- **Who**: Entire staff

- **When**: As per the organizational campaign calendar

Campaign Definition and Goals for Leadership Communication

The goal of the Microsoft Communication Sites Literacy Campaign is to increase the literacy of the Microsoft communication sites among all staff, make them excited and develop confidence to work with it, enable them to make decisions using communication sites' data, and accelerate their organizational digital journeys. The campaign supports a culture where data entry into Microsoft communication sites is a value-added activity, a culture with a reusable mentality, and where data is owned and trusted.

What Does a Digitally Literate Staff Look Like?

Know

- **Meaning**: Know the value of communication sites, their health, how to use them and where to find them.

- **Case for change**: The case for change is to accelerate the digital transformation.

- **Impact**: How can you create value from this and support new business models.

- **Principles**: Make contributions to communication sites everyone's responsibility. Data is governed in line with the enterprise information and security policy.

Feel

- **The need**: Understand the urgency of the digital transformation and use communication sites for knowledge and content management purposes.

- **The value**: See high-quality data inside communication sites, this has clear value for users, businesses, and the organization.

- **The confidence:** The organization is excited and confident about how data in the communication sites is a competitive differentiator and how this data can help the organization stay relevant.

Do

- **Culture**: Embrace Microsoft communication sites in day-to-today activities.

- **Learn:** Be eager to share lessons.

- **Treat**: Treat data in communication sites as an asset and keep it safe and secure.

- **Articulate**: Describe the organizational drivers and the benefits of digital transformation using communication sites.

- **Apply**: A communication site data mindset, being able to read, contribute, and discuss data in different context.

Now that you have some knowledge of the goals of this campaign, let's be practical and distinguish between good and bad communication sites.

Measuring the Success of Adoption

To measure success, you must distinguish between good communication site literacy and bad communication site literacy.

Good communication site literacy:

- Examining sites in in Microsoft communication sites and making a decision

- Having a formal communication sites literacy strategy, program, and plan

- Commissioning value-based dashboards; checking on usage with the help of Power BI

- Common understanding of communication sites features

- Understanding, articulating, and using communication sites in relation to a business case; seeking the relevant data, internally/externally, and structured/ unstructured

- Telling succinct, but thorough data stories

- Viewing and treating communication sites as an enterprise asset

- Focusing on high-value diagnostic, predictive, and prescriptive analytics

- Consider communication sites skills during hiring, performance reviews, and learning, and development

- Integrating with standalone and non-Microsoft repositories

- Leadership by example; they are visible and are the communication sites champions

Bad communication site literacy:

- Cherry-picking data to justify a decision

- Saying that communication sites data is important, but not treating it as such

- Making reports as "that's the way we've always done it"

- Inconsistent understanding of communication sites data terminology; silos

- Not understanding communication sites data in a business context; using data from other systems because it's available/easy to use; not seeking more suitable data

- Misleading by using the wrong chart type or measure for a dataset

- Representing conclusions without adequate context – fake news!

- Individuals/departments hoarding communication sites, limiting their value to others

- Focus on reporting and analyzing past activity only

- Not considering communication site competencies in new hires

- Minimal analytics infrastructure

- Good Communication site behaviors not exhibited or championed

Let's now look at how good and bad communication site literacy differs.

Appearance of Good Communication Sites Literacy

In general:

- Explicitly call out communication sites as important

- Communication sites have known and visible sponsors

- Leadership demonstrates behavior using communication sites

- Project communication sites is not viewed as a by-product; reporting and analytics are not afterthoughts

- Formal strategy, program, and plan for communication sites

- Existence of communication sites glossary, catalogue, and dictionary

- Communication sites knowledge is incorporated into hiring and performance

- Communication sites data is trusted and understood

- Meetings cover how communication sites, metrics, and analytics can be leveraged to demonstrate business value

- A commonly heard phrase is: "What does the communication sites data tell us?"

For consumers of communication sites:

- Ability to describe the communication sites data, metrics, and analysis used in a business use case

- Ask good questions of communication sites

- Hypothesis test with communication sites

- Distinguish correlation from causality using communication sites

- Understand the value of communication sites as an asset

- The power of blending types and sources from communication sites

- Adherence to communication sites data privacy, security, ethics, bias, and risk

- Adopt self-service business intelligence using communication sites

- Active, engaged data storytelling using knowledge centers

- Variety of analytical techniques using communication sites

For communication sites data contributors:

- Communication sites data quality understood by those who enter/create data

- Common communication sites data language – not silos

- Analytics professionals can articulate varying communication sites management approaches

- Data-discovery and augmented analytics capabilities and tools are in place and used

- Opportunistic embedding of communication sites into business workflow to make faster decisions

- Use of communication sites for visualization and storytelling

- Integration with standalone repositories to derive value from content

- Development programs in place to attract, develop, manage, and retain top talent

- Certification in place or in development for communication sites

Appearance of Bad Communication Sites Literacy

In general:

- No common language – e.g., metadata repository being referred to as and understood to be a derivation from communication sites

- All talk – talking about the importance of communication sites data, but not treating it as important

- Creating and funding dashboards without vetting their usage and value

- Failure to consider the communication sites competencies of new hires in any position

- Not understanding how to articulate business impact and actual contribution to business value using communication sites

- A rarely heard phrase is: "What does the data tell us?"

For consumers of communication sites:

- Cherry-picking data to justify a decision, not examining the data to inform a decision

- Not clarifying or challenging assumptions

- Saying "Give me the data and I will figure out what to do with it later"; using Microsoft communication sites just because it's what you have available

- Using wrong terminologies to explain Microsoft communication sites

- Asking for a report because "that's the way we've always done it"

- Not identifying and adjusting for inherent or implicit biases

- Idle project repositories for many years

- Fake news: Representing Microsoft communication sites and conclusions in a way that does not provide adequate context, clarification of assumptions, and/or discerning interrogation by the viewers

For Microsoft Communication Sites Contributors:

- Relying on internal structured data because it is familiar and easy to access, rather than exploring other relevant internal and external data sources and types such as Microsoft communication sites

- Not treating information as an enterprise asset, e.g., individuals and departments hoarding data, thus limiting its value to others

- High-value diagnostic, predictive, and prescriptive analytics over Microsoft communication sites

- Narrow/local focus; failing to consider other ways to monetize information internally and externally from communication sites

- Lack of professional development and certification programs related to Microsoft communication sites

After defining the campaign goals and the definition, you need to define the campaign's scope. It is comprised of three phases—let's get started, let's do it, and embed it.

The Literacy Awareness Campaign Scope

Phase 1 focusses on aspects of user awareness.

Phase 1. Let's Get Started

- Define basic topics to know about Microsoft's communication sites.

- Define learning paths for end users and super users.

- Define most the valued internal professional (MVP) for the communication sites.

- Curate content for normal a communication sites user.

- Create extra MVP content.

- Define a strategy and approach.

Phase 2. Let's Do It

- Complete the existing content (internal and external) for MVP.

- Complete the extra MVP content.

- Create the communication site's literacy SharePoint.

- Create the MVP learning paths.

- Identify the communications contacts per segment.

- Pilot the MVP.

Phase 3. Embed It

- Curate the remaining existing content (internal and external).

- Create the remaining extra content.

- Create the remaining learning paths.

- Create the communications content.

- Create and share the communications plan with the segment contacts.

During any campaign roll-out, there are pain points. Probable pain points are different competencies to adopt communication sites, lack of business value, lack of reward and recognition, and lack of support.

Pain points in a Microsoft Communication Literacy Campaign

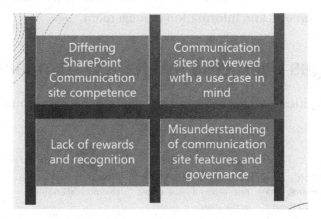

Figure 2-5. *Pain points of a literacy campaign*

The following bullets explain each area of Figure 2-5:

- Differing Microsoft communication sites competence to adopt organization wide

- Communication sites are not viewed with a use case in mind. Data journeys inside communication sites through the supply chain are not understood.

- There are no incentives/penalties for staff for adoption or participation (i.e. no reward and recognition program).

- Communication sites' management, controls, and governance are not understood or prioritized; they are seen as low value and high effort. There is a proliferation of multiple versions of the truth.

Initially, the literacy campaign is about building awareness at scale and increasing understanding of the importance of the communication sites. Later initiatives can build on this to address specific areas, such as knowledge, content, and information management.

Challenges Overcome by Literacy Campaigns

The opportunities outlined in Figure 2-6 can be achieved through literacy campaigns.

Opportunity	Business Blocker	Literacy Campaign Achievement
Available Microsoft **communication** sites data **and** why **you** need **them**	Communication sites are not seen as a value-added application Limited understanding of communication sites and their data	Awareness on the value of data in the communication sites Increase adoption of communication sites
Predictive, diagnostic, prescriptive, information Data-driven decision making	Data created without a use case in mind Inconsistent categorization Disconnected systems	Awareness of the data lifecycle and the importance of quality data inside communication sites Changed mindset for effective management of content
Data-driven decision making	Unable to articulate questions that could be solved using data available in communication sites Can't discern relevant data from communication sites	Solving business problems with information coming from communication sites Identifying business value with data from communication sites Visualization and storytelling from information coming from communication sites
Innovation based on information-derived insights from Project Cortes	Unable to articulate questions that could be solved using information coming from communication sites Can't discern relevant data	Developed understanding that everyone has a role to play, and the importance of the "right" point of entry Improved access to get suitable data from communication sites

Figure 2-6. *Opportunities achieved through literacy campaigns*

The last step of any campaign is measuring its success. Measuring engagement with the campaign is critical, as it gives you insights into which communities or users are engaging most/least. See Figure 2-7.

SharePoint analytics	Use out-of-the-box SharePoint analytics to track metrics such as which materials were clicked, and the frequency and duration of engagement.
Video views	Track views, likes, and shares on campaign videos; use this information to determine which modules are most popular, and which could be advertised more.
Communication site success stories	As part of the campaign, encourage people to share how they have applied their new knowledge. Track how many of these stories are received.
Embedding elsewhere	Embedding literacy materials into other training is a key part of the campaign and will be one measure of success.
Feedback surveys	A feedback survey could be set up, both for the communication sites' pilot groups, and for a cross-section of end users, to learn what they like and what could be improved.
Yammer interaction	Yammer is a core platform for sharing the communication sites literacy materials. Interaction on Yammer will be a useful indicator of campaign engagement.
Goals and KPIs	If information coming from the communication sites related to KPIs/GPAs can be implemented across the business, you can track success against these long-term.

Figure 2-7. Measuring a campaign

Summary

This chapter explained how to roll out different techniques to create user awareness, launch communication site campaigns, and create intelligent and informed communities. The primarily focus was on creating user awareness, creating plans for implementation, executing campaigns, and measuring the success of adoption. The next chapter covers information compliance and governance aspects of communication sites, as the global user community falls into different zones where information has been classified at different levels.

CHAPTER 3

Building Collaborative Experiences for End Users

After exploring techniques for effective communication and collaboration, you can make them feasible with seamless integration between Microsoft Teams or Teams and SharePoint communication sites. The focus of this chapter is as follows:

- An introduction to Teams

- Teams' end user features

- Teams' outstanding features

- How to make the most of Teams

- Seamless integration between SharePoint communication sites and Teams

- Seamless integration between SharePoint communication sites and Power BI

© Charles David Waghmare 2023
C. D. Waghmare, *Beginning SharePoint Communication Sites*,
https://doi.org/10.1007/978-1-4842-8960-0_3

An introduction to MS Teams

Microsoft Teams is a productivity platform that combines various forms of communication, such as video meetings, apps, documents, and chat, to create a unified interface. Organizations can work on projects and topics in one place. Chats are also a great way for groups to keep up with their conversations, as they provide threaded discussions.

This chapter covers how to use Microsoft Teams. It's available to all of Microsoft's 365 customers, including businesses, education, and government licenses. Just have your network administrator turn on the Team app.

With Microsoft Teams, you can easily create and manage a group that's made up of people from different backgrounds. There are a variety of tools that you can use to help your groups work together, such as Excel, PowerPoint, and Word.

One of Microsoft Teams' best features is its ability to organize all of the resources that your team members use, such as documents, notes, and photos. With the ability to bring in other apps, such as Twitter and Bing News, you can easily organize content in one place.

In 2018, Microsoft started onboarding all new M365 customers under 500 seats using Skype for Business into Teams. The chat functionality of the app remains the same, but it's only available in the cloud. Most of the people who were previously using Skype for Business have switched to Teams.

With Microsoft Teams, you can rest assured that your data is protected from various security threats. It features a variety of features that help keep your team members and their data secure. Some of these include two-factor authentication and encryption.

The ability to adapt your workspace to meet the needs of your team is also a great feature of Microsoft Teams. It can be used to create and manage a variety of features that are designed to help your team members work more efficiently. One such feature is the ability to connect to third-party vendors.

The ability to work on different platforms is also a great feature of Microsoft Teams. It can be used on various devices, such as Windows 10, Mac, iOS, Android, and Windows Phones. The app is very intuitive to use once it's enabled.

Although Microsoft Teams is a great collaboration tool, it's not the first of its kind. Other tools, such as Google's Slack and Webex Teams, also exist.

A quick look at the various features of Microsoft Teams and Slack shows that they have similar features. However, with the native integration of Microsoft apps, you can work on files within the app instead of using other tools, such as Slack.

If you're a Microsoft 365 customer, it's no longer a good idea to use other collaboration tools because the full functionality of Team is already available to you.

Team's End User Features

Since Microsoft Teams was introduced in 2017, it has been gaining widespread popularity. It's a cloud-based communication platform that replaces the traditional business software, such as Skype for Business. Employees can participate in group messaging, audio calls, and video meetings.

The Teams service is a part of Microsoft 365, and it can be used with other productivity tools such as Word, Excel, and Outlook. If you're already using these tools, it's a great fit. Here are just some of Team's features:

- Chat feature with one-to-one chat and group chat

- Message threads

- Emojis, GIFs, and stickers

- Multifactor authentication

- Channel favoriting and following

- @Mentions

- Activity feed

- Integration with third-party tools

- Meeting scheduling

- Audio conferencing

- File sharing

- Screen sharing

- Alerts

- Assistant bots

- Contact search

- Organization hierarchy

- Conversation search

Teams is designed to improve the flow of information in your company. It can help you keep track of all of your important details and make sure that everyone is communicating effectively.

According to a blog post by Nick Stein, 86 percent of employees cite the lack of collaboration as a reason for their company's failure. With Microsoft Teams, you can easily implement a strategy that will help improve your team's efficiency. Let's look at some features that drive your organization goals.

Teams Connect

In March 2021, Microsoft introduced Teams Connect (see Figure 3-1), a feature that lets organizations share channels with other organizations. It is similar to Slack Connect.

Figure 3-1. *Partner channel*

Federation with Slack or Webex

Some of the best teams apps are those that are typically viewed as competitors. Do you ever communicate with people outside of your organization?

According to some studies, people tend to use apps other than Microsoft Teams when it comes to communicating with colleagues. For instance, they might use Slack or Cisco Webex. If this is the case, it can be very unproductive to switch from Teams to another app, especially if you're trying to start a new conversation.

Unfortunately, many people end up using email instead of other apps when they need to communicate with colleagues. To address this issue, Mio has created a universal channel for Microsoft Teams that allows you to chat with other teams using Webex or Slack (see Figure 3-2).

Figure 3-2. Federation between Webex and Slack

You can easily send messages to your suppliers, contractors, and clients who use Webex or Slack using Microsoft Teams. The messages will stay in the app while Mio translates them across the platform. Besides messages, the universal channels for Microsoft Teams also support various other messaging apps, such as emojis, files, and channels. If you're a fan of this type of app, you can easily install it and start creating channels for free.

Teams Tab: Static and Configurable

The best apps for Microsoft Teams are built into the platform. There are two kinds of tabs in the app: one for interactive content and one for rich web content (see Figure 3-3).

Figure 3-3. *Teams tab*

Static tabs support individual users. Configurable tabs, on the other hand, are part of your Teams channel and provide ongoing guidance and information.

Immersive reader

One of the most underutilized features of Microsoft Teams is the immersive reader, which allows users to speak text on a channel at varying speeds. This capability is useful if you are having a hard time focusing on a particular piece of text. Click on the three dots of any message and select Immersive Reader from the menu to access this feature (see Figure 3-4).

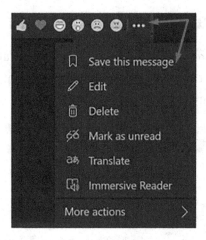

Figure 3-4. *The Immersive Reader feature*

Filter Content Using @mention

It's hard to keep up with the latest news in Microsoft Teams when your eyes are constantly on the live chat feed. Fortunately, you can easily filter the content that you see with the @mentions feature.

This feature lets you separate your personal messages from other topics that are not relevant. It also helps keep you up-to-date with the latest information (see Figure 3-5).

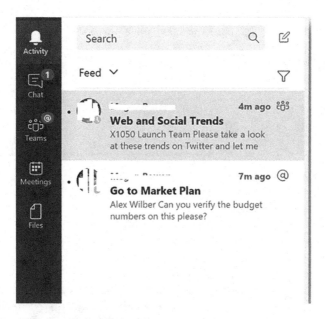

Figure 3-5. *Filter using @mention*

Bookmarking

When you need to find the information quickly, Microsoft Teams can help you keep track of all the content you need. You can easily classify content into different categories so that you can spend less time searching for important data (see Figure 3-6).

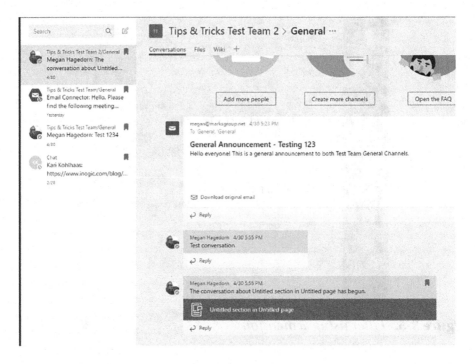

Figure 3-6. *Bookmarking in Teams*

Being able to keep track of all details in a chat app is also very important. Having a well-defined and organized view of all of your content helps you find the information that you need.

Slash Commands

Today's fast-paced workplace requires employees to work as efficiently as possible. One of the most important factors when it comes to improving productivity is making sure that employees can navigate through Microsoft Teams easily and intuitively.

One of the easiest ways to do this is by using the slash command. For instance, you can set your status to "online" or "away". You can also make sure that you're not missing out on any new features by going to the Release Notes tab of the T-bot channel.

The /Files feature shows the most recent files that you've shared with Microsoft Teams. /GoTo opens a channel in which you can easily jump to a specific area. /Help sends a message to someone else through the T-bot.

Meeting Whiteboards

Microsoft Teams members can now access a whiteboard in the app. There, they can create sketches and share ideas. Participants can choose from a variety of pen colors and graph options (see Figure 3-7).

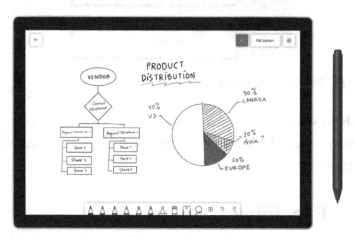

Figure 3-7. *Whiteboarding in MS Teams*

You can now collaborate with other people using Microsoft Teams and the Whiteboard app. Both tools allow you to share and draw content in real-time. The app for tablets and pens also has a tab that allows people to write with their fingers.

Private Channels

With the ability to create private channels in Teams (see Figure 3-8), you can control how people collaborate and communicate with each other. This feature is useful for financial firms, as certain parts of the organization may not be allowed to see and share information.

Figure 3-8. *Private channels*

The ability to create private channels in Teams was first previewed at Enterprise Connect. This feature makes it easier for people to control how their data is shared. See Figure 3-8.

Meeting Recording

One of the most effective ways to keep track of important information is by recording Microsoft Teams meetings.

During a meeting, audio, video, and screen sharing activities are captured at the same time. They can then be saved to Stream, which allows you to access them later (see Figure 3-9).

Figure 3-9. *Teams recording with compliance*

If you're planning on creating company-wide announcements or releasing news items, recording meetings is a great way to do it. You can also create training videos for your employees by clicking the Start Recording button in the channel.

Integration with PSTN

You can now integrate the Microsoft Teams experience with the public switched telephone network (PSTN). There are various ways to do this, such as through direct routing or through the Microsoft Calling Plans. The cloud-based subscription allows you to use the calling plans without additional hardware.

If your business wants to use the Microsoft Teams experience but still use the existing PTSN trunk, you can use Direct Routing. This method works with any telephony provider and allows you to connect to the cloud-based service. However, you will need a session border controller to use this method.

Teams Bot

If you're a business that wants to take advantage of the various features of the Microsoft Teams experience, such as automation and artificial intelligence, then try the pre-made bots.

There are many types of bots (see Figure 3-10) that can be useful for your business, such as Polly, which is a simple bot that lets you poll your team members. Who Bot is a chatbot that can help you keep track of your team members' engagement. Grow Bot is a feature that lets team members exchange ideas. Stats bot is an analytics bot that can deliver scheduled reports through Google Analytics.

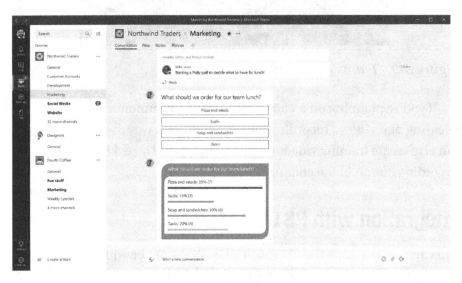

Figure 3-10.   *The Teams bots*

Hard Audio Mute

The goal of a learning environment is to reduce distractions. With hard audio mute, attendees can't interrupt the meeting. This tool is ideal for education and enterprise settings.

From the participant pane, you can mute all participants. Administrators can also remove the hard mute setting when someone raises their hand to contribute. This feature ensures that the interactions between participants (such as students and teachers) are secure and uninterrupted. Additionally, student lobbies allow educators to control when students join a meeting.

Team Live Events

Teams can host live events for large audiences, such as conferences and meetings, through its platform. It's a convenient way to ask everyone to join a meeting.

Event organizers can set the permissions for the attendees and co-presenters, and they can also share the screens and windows of their broadcasts (see Figure 3-11).

Figure 3-11. *Teams Live event*

Recording with Automatic Transcripts

Today's fast-paced world often prevents people from remembering important details about their meetings. With the help of cloud recording and automatic transcription, you can keep track of all of your meetings and keep them in the cloud.

With the help of automatic transcription (see Figure 3-12), you can easily go back and listen to all of your conversations with your team. It also makes it easier to find important information, because you can do so by just typing a phrase or keyword.

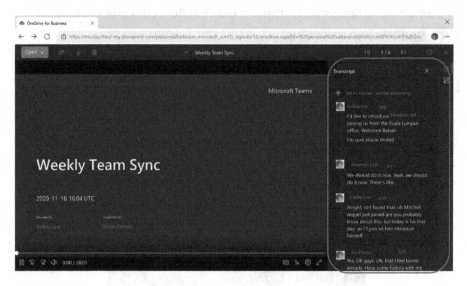

Figure 3-12. *Recordings with scripts*

With these awesome features, Teams has become a popular collaborative platform. During the COVID-19 pandemic, many companies adopted Teams for their employees to collaborate on business activities when working from home.

How to Make the Most of Teams

Microsoft Teams is a great way to keep your company connected, especially when your workers are away from the office. The following sections include a variety of tips that will help you get organized and make the most of the Teams app.

Simplicity

One of the biggest advantages of using Microsoft Teams is its ability to integrate with other tools. For example, you can add a Teams site to the platform by using the SharePoint extension. This can be done through the Team site's list and pages. You can also add documents and full sites from the Website tab.

One of the most important steps that you should take when creating a group post is to add a subject title to it. This will make it easier for people to keep track of the group's activities. Creating a fun team environment can also help people get used to the platform.

Use the Teams Mobile App

To enable teamwork on the go, download the Microsoft Teams app. It will allow you to set boundaries and monitor your work time.

Maintain and Optimize Lists of Teams

One of the most important factors that you should consider when it comes to starting a new team is the number of channels that it should have. Having a large team with dedicated channels allows you to collaborate on various projects and topics. Don't confuse your team with the roles they play. Having several large groups with multiple channels will allow you to enable more effective teamwork.

Regularly Update Channels

One of the most important factors that you should consider when it comes to creating a new team is the number of channels that it should have. Having multiple channels will allow you to pull together all of your related content into one place. There is a learning curve when it comes to this, but by adding files to each channel, everyone can easily find them and use them.

Make Use of Team Apps

Microsoft Teams has a variety of features that can be used to enhance the efficiency of your team, such as the ability to integrate various tools. One of the most fun features that can be used is the ability to create a badge that will allow you to recognize the achievements of your team.

Manage Content

Getting organized can be hard if users aren't careful, so use tools such as OneNote or Wiki to keep conversations simple and focused. These features can help highlight important content and keep conversations flowing smoothly.

Highlight Important Resources

You can easily add multiple websites that track various aspects of a site's performance, including news, performance, and live site monitoring. To do so, highlight the + and select Tab. These websites will automatically appear at the top of a channel.

You can also pin your favorite channels and chats to the top of your list. To do so, select the three dots beside the group and then select Pin. This will keep your most important conversations and channels at the top.

Forward Email Conversations

You can easily forward an email to a group in Teams so that it can receive faster feedback. To do so, go to the ellipsis menu, select Get Email Address, and then click Copy. In Outlook, open the app and paste the email address you want to forward to your channel into the To field.

Keep Channels Active

It takes discipline to get organized, but it will be worth it if you are following the proper channels and engaging in conversations. Use the following instructions to keep conversations flowing smoothly.

Have Fun

Microsoft Teams is a great tool for working with your colleagues. It features everything you need to keep conversations flowing smoothly. You can use it to send and receive virtual happy hours, make calls with background images, and more.

Where Should You Store Files? In Teams or on a SharePoint Communication Site?

The Microsoft Teams platform is a hub for teamwork that allows people to work together seamlessly. It includes a variety of features such as chat, meetings, and documents. Its sibling, the Microsoft 365 platform, is an intranet that enables people to store, share, and communicate information across various platforms.

When you create a new team, a Microsoft 365 Group, Exchange Online, and other services such as Power BI and Calendar are automatically created as well. The documents that you share with your team are stored in a site that's created to store them. This is different from what happens in Microsoft Teams.

The exact location of the files that you share with a team can vary depending on the channel that they're in. For instance, if you create a General channel, the files that you share with that channel are stored in the Documents library inside the General folder (see Figure 3-13). On the other hand, if you create a Team channel called Project A, the files that you share with that channel are stored in the Project A folder. This applies to all standard channels in Microsoft Teams. Private channels, on the other hand, have their own architecture that allows them to have separate sites and different permissions. More information about these channels can be found in the official documentation of Microsoft Teams (see Figure 3-14).

Figure 3-13. *Files under the General tab*

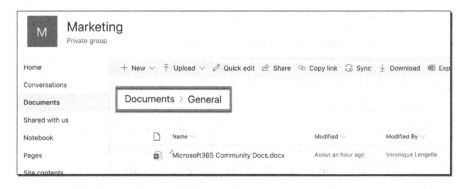

Figure 3-14. *Files under a private channel*

You can access your files in different ways depending on the interface that you prefer. For instance, you can access them in Microsoft Teams or through the web-based version of Microsoft Office. However, if you want to perform more advanced settings, you'll need to go to the desktop version of Microsoft Office.

The easiest way to access your files in Microsoft Teams is through the Files tab located at the top. This interface is similar to that of a SharePoint communication site. It allows you to create new files, browse through all of your documents, and download or upload them.

You can also open the associated site in Microsoft Teams by clicking on the ellipses icon (...) in the top-right corner of the channel that you're in. If you're in the Posts tab of a channel, you can click the ellipses icon (...)in the to- right corner and select Open the Associated SharePoint Site.

Security trimming is applied to all files in Microsoft 365. Users can only view and search content that they have access to, which is respected by both Microsoft Teams and the web-based version of Microsoft Office, known as SharePoint Online. When you remove or add a user to a team, their access to the associated site is also removed or added.

All of your files and documents are saved wherever you are, regardless of which version of Microsoft Office you're using. You can always update the latest version of the document in Microsoft Teams and in SharePoint communication sites.

Seamless Integration Between SharePoint Communication Sites and Teams

Teams is a collaboration hub that brings various Microsoft apps together into one place. However, the relationship between those apps and the communication sites can get confusing. Many people may not know which tool to use, or even if they need both. The good news is that Teams and communication sites work together seamlessly.

Files and Chats

Teams and communication sites are two different platforms, but with the ability to manage documents in both Teams and in communication sites, team members can work together seamlessly. With the help of its single document library, known as OneDrive for Business, you can store and manage all of your documents in one place.

Files in a private chat using Teams can be stored in the Microsoft Team Chat Files directory. This is because the permissions and archiving of the cloud-based platform allow users to store and manage all of their files in one place.

Although it's possible to use Teams without using a communication site, users can then only share files in standard channels. Also, users can't access private chats (see Figure 3-15) with the help of OneDrive for Business.

Figure 3-15. *Document library in a Teams channel*

With Teams, users can collaborate and communicate using video meetings and other forms of communication. SharePoint communication sites are used to store and manage all of your documents (see Figure 3-16).

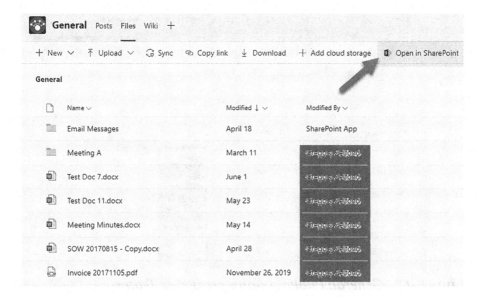

Figure 3-16. *The same document library on a SharePoint communication site*

Document Management System, SharePoint Communication Sites and Teams

Every team in Microsoft has a communication site that includes a document library. The files that are created or uploaded to a team are stored in the library, not on the team's site. Even if you upload files to a team, those files are still accessible in both applications.

The default channel for a team is General, which prevents it from being renamed or deleted (see Figure 3-17). Files that are stored in this channel are stored in the General library of the communication site.

Figure 3-17.   *General: Public channel created in Teams*

When you create a new public channel in Teams, a corresponding folder is created in the document library (see Figure 3-18).

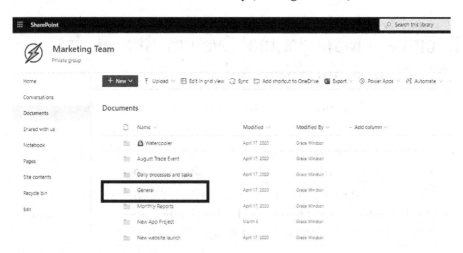

Figure 3-18.   *General folder created in document library*

The name and file path of the channel are based on the channel name. Although you can change its name, the underlying path remains the same.

A *private channel* is a different kind of channel. It features a separate document library and a lightweight site collection. Only members of the team are allowed to access it. Non-members will not be aware it exists.

Before you start a private channel, make sure that it's not a public channel. It can be created and operated by a private team, which offers a better alternative if you have specific requirements. As part of its permissions structure, Teams uses the security trimming found in Microsoft 365.

Users can easily access their content through the private channel. When a user is added to or removed from a team, they gain or lose their access to the communication site's documents.

Work with Attachments in Teams

Microsoft is working on a way to make it easier for people to manage their documents in Teams using the Files tab in the main site. If you're already familiar with the features of the SharePoint communication site, you should be able to easily start using this new feature.

The Files tab in Teams (see Figure 3-19) can be used to find and manage all of your documents. You can also filter results by file type, team, and modified by. To do so, go to the left-side navigation and click the Files button.

Figure 3-19. *Access all files part of entire Teams*

The Files tab in Teams allows you to upload existing files and folders. You can create a new folder or move folder to a new location. You can also sync them to your desktop for quicker access. With the click of a button, you can open, copy, and save files in Teams or anywhere.

In real-time, you can co-edit documents and start a conversation. You can also add comments to a document, and you can click the Pin to Top button to add important files to a library. You can also list documents as tabs in a channel so they can easily be found.

With a comprehensive document management solution, your team members can work on projects regardless of where they are located.

Seamless Integration Between SharePoint Communication Sites and Power BI

Microsoft Power BI is a business intelligence and data visualization tool that can be used to analyze and visualize complex data. It includes various software services and apps that help users get the most out of their data.

Before you can move data from Microsoft's SharePoint to Power BI, you need to have the necessary prerequisites. These include the Power BI Desktop app and the license list for the library.

In order to get the data from the library or list from the SharePoint communication sites, you need to embed data in Power BI. This will then be integrated into the report.

The first step in this process is to download and install the Power BI Desktop app. After that, go to the Home tab and click the Get Data button. There, you can also view the various options in the drop-down menu.

From the drop-down menu, click the More button (see Figure 3-20). The Get Data dialog box will appear in the search bar. Three options will appear; choose the list or the library in Microsoft's SharePoint (see Figure 3-21).

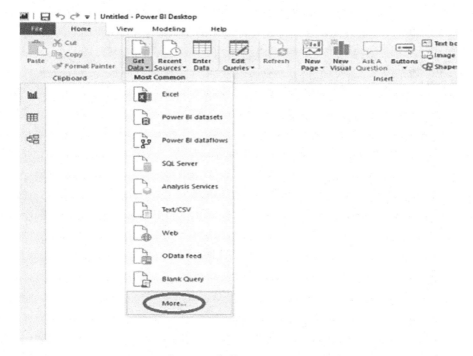

Figure 3-20. *Get Data from a different source such as SharePoint*

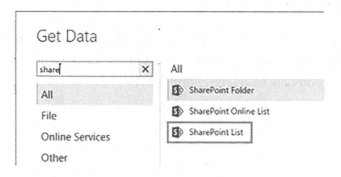

Figure 3-21. *Choose SharePoint List*

After selecting SharePoint List, you need to load the data. Go to the Power BI Desktop app and click the Load button. This will allow you to create a report that will be presented in Power BI (see Figure 3-22).

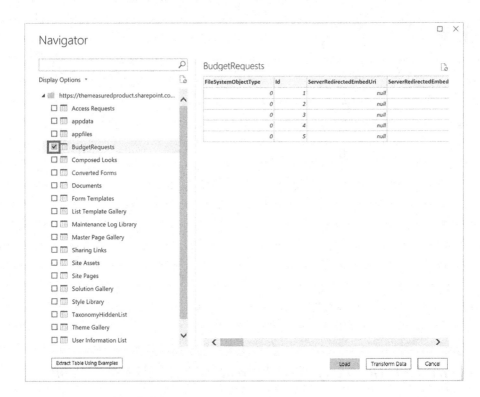

Figure 3-22. *Load data in Power BI*

To create a SharePoint list report in Power BI, you need to fetch data from the SharePoint list. To do that, access the home page of the Power BI desktop app and data icon (see Figure 3-23)

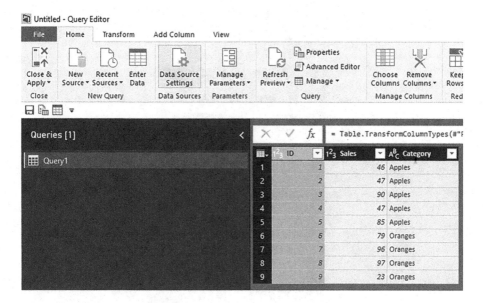

Figure 3-23.   *Fetch data from SharePoint list into Power BI*

Select the columns that you want to visualize and, with the help of the Visualizations pane (see Figure 3-24), use the features to display the data.

Figure 3-24. *Data visualizations pane*

Another way to create a report is by accessing the Integrate menu under a document library or list in the communication sites, as shown in Figure 3-25.

Figure 3-25. Access the Integrate menu from a document library

Power BI reports in communication sites can also be created using the Power BI webpart, as shown in Figure 3-26.

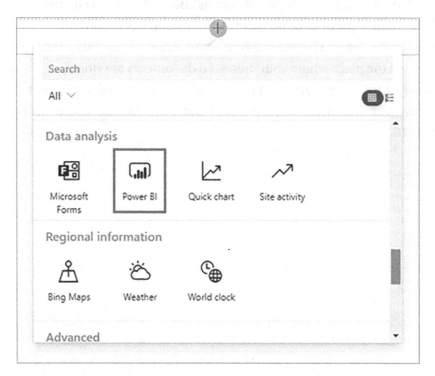

Figure 3-26. Power BI webpart

You must first add a webpart to a page in order to configure it. The link to the Power BI report will be known to you, and then the communication page will be rendered automatically with a Power BI report.

This is a simple and fast way to integrate Power BI with SharePoint communication sites. It allows you to visualize large amounts of data in a way that's easy to understand. Also, you don't need to move between platforms to get the most out of the reports.

Summary

This chapter introduced Microsoft Teams and explained its end user features and some of its outstanding features, such as Recording Compliance, Teams Live Events, Immersive Reader, and others. We identified the place where your uploaded documents are stored, and this place is simply communication sites. Finally, at the end of the chapter, you saw seamless integration between communication sites, Teams, and Power BI.

CHAPTER 4

Creating Digital Intranets

After learning about collaboration with Teams and communication sites in the last chapter, this chapter focuses on the digital aspects of communication sites. In this chapter, you will look at intranets and learn why intranets can be crucial to executing day-to-day work tasks. You'll also learn to create a visually appealing intranet using simple communication site features.

The term *digital workplace* refers to a work environment that is more complex than an intranet. It's not a replacement for an existing intranet, nor is it a replacement for an enterprise portal. Instead, it's a collection of tools that allow people to get work done.

Many people claim that they were the first to define or use the term digital workplace. Consultants love to argue that they are the first to coin a phrase or combination of words that have, in fact, been around for a long time. The reality is that the term has been used in various forms and languages for a long time. I first heard it in 2002 when IBM referred its internal environment as a digital workplace.

Unfortunately, there are many consultant-speak terms that refer to the digital workplace that are not only misleading, but also inappropriate. For instance, one consultant definition says that it's a consumer-like environment that enables flexible working and innovative ideas.

C. D. Waghmare, *Beginning SharePoint Communication Sites*,
https://doi.org/10.1007/978-1-4842-8960-0_4

The rise of the digital workplace has been attributed to the increasing popularity of its ability to improve employee experience and productivity. It's also a great alternative to the traditional office space. More and more organizations are implementing this type of work environment.

While the digital workplace is commonly referred to as a replacement for an existing intranet, this type of work environment has been around for a long time and has evolved to meet the needs of today's workforce. Although it's easy to assume that the two platforms are the same, they are actually two different tools that can be used together to improve the efficiency of an organization.

An *intranet* is a type of private network that enables employees to communicate and collaborate. Modern versions of these networks focus more on the employee experience. They also aim to provide more integration and personalization features to make it easier for workers to manage their work.

Over the years, the intranet has been the place where employees store and access their data. Now, it's become more organized and provides a more secure environment for storing and accessing data.

The main repository of all company data, an intranet helps employees work together and efficiently. It also supports the culture of the organization by allowing members to communicate effectively.

A digital workplace is a type of workplace that enables employees to access all the necessary tools and resources to perform their everyday tasks. It eliminates the need for the physical office and allows them to work more efficiently. This type of environment also allows them to integrate all the different applications used by the company.

A digital workplace can help employees work more efficiently and effectively by allowing them to collaborate with other team members. It can also automate various repetitive tasks and improve the efficiency of their business processes.

The modern intranet is often referred to as a dashboard of a digital workplace. It serves as the central hub for all company communication and information. Your company's tools, such as process management and project management, can be used from an intranet to facilitate collaboration and work management. An intranet can also help enhance the customer and employee experiences.

The design of an intranet allows employees to feel part of the organization, as it serves as the central hub for all company communication. It can also be a great way to store important documents.

An Intranet Is Necessary for Digital Workplaces

The more applications that you use, the more time that employees spend switching between them, which will only decrease their efficiency and overwhelm them. There are also various other factors that can affect the efficiency of your organization, such as multiple logins and handling of data.

Through the use of an intranet, you can get a centralized view of all the data in an organization, allowing you to access all the business tools and information that you need. You would only have to log in to the intranet to get full access to these features. The goal of using an intranet as an identity provider is to make it easy for employees to log in to different applications.

The digital workplace has a huge amount of data that organizations can store and manage. Without the proper search capabilities, they would not have the necessary knowledge to use it efficiently.

An intranet can be built with the necessary integration to allow users to easily access all the information that they need from the various parts of the digital workplace. With a simple search bar, an intranet can become the enterprise Google for your company. It can also be used to find employee or company-related content.

An intranet is built with the necessary features to help employees find the right information at the right time, which will improve their experience and increase their productivity. With the help of social features, integration, and user-friendly interfaces, an intranet can transform the way employees interact with the digital workplace.

The main gateway to the digital workplace is an intranet, which is a highly functional and versatile platform that can be used to extend and improve the communication and digital strategies of an organization. It can also be used to create and manage various applications. There is no need to choose between the two, as both platforms can be used to their fullest.

Differences Between a Digital Workplace and an Intranet

When it comes to choosing the right digital workplace or intranet solution for your business, the difference is important to understand. Since the pandemic forced many companies to rethink their approach to communication, many of them have turned to digital workplace and intranet solutions to help their employees work from anywhere.

What is an intranet and how does it differ from a digital workplace? The main difference between an intranet and a digital workplace is their purpose. Also, the communication and collaboration capabilities of both solutions are different.

Intranets used to be dumping grounds for outdated technology. If we had had more images of tumbleweeds, we would have had a lot of home page content.

Today, intranets are used to create powerful communication platforms. There are a variety of features that are commonly featured in modern intranets, such as data dashboards, notice boards, and social media feeds.

The concept of a digital workplace refers to the various technologies that people use to get work done today. Some of these include email, instant messaging, and social media.

The term *digital workplace* refers to the environment where all of your digital tools are located. An intranet is a microenvironment within the digital workplace, where various tools are stored, as shown in Figure 4-1.

There are a lot of misunderstandings about the terms digital workplace and intranet. Digital workplace is often used to describe platforms that allow people to store and share knowledge. On the other hand, intranet is often used to describe a place where communication and collaboration can take place.

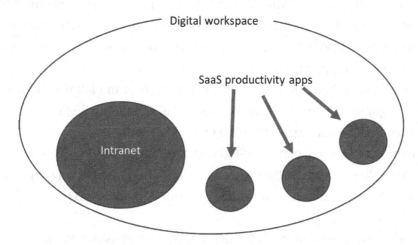

Figure 4-1. *The difference between digital workspaces and Intranets*

The Purpose of an Intranet

An intranet is a final destination that allows employees to share their content and services with the rest of the organization. It serves as a repository for all the company's policies and procedures, as well as for news and events. It also features a variety of tools that allow employees to manage their various business processes.

The marketing team can use the intranet to store their latest and final materials. This eliminates a lot of pressure and helps sales and customer service staff members find the materials they need quickly. They can also use it to keep track of the latest versions of their marketing materials, which helps them respond quickly to any situation.

The HR department is responsible for managing and informing employees about all of the company's policies and procedures. Having the latest versions of the software on the intranet makes it easier for managers to keep track of all of the latest changes. This also helps employees keep up with the changes in the industry.

Through self-service, employees can log in to their various tasks and requests, such as holiday and IT problems, and fill out expense forms. This eliminates a lot of pressure and helps the department respond quickly to any situation. It also helps them get rid of backlogs caused by the increased activity of their employees.

This can also help reduce the department's costs and allow it to focus on other goals. In an ideal world, it would be easier for the department to focus on creative and innovation projects.

Through the use of company-led initiatives on the intranet, you can receive feedback from the entire organization. This is a great way to get in touch with the people who are working at your company and provide them with valuable insight.

One of the most important factors that you can consider when it comes to implementing company-led initiatives is the development of effective communication. This can be done through the use of two-way communication, which ensures that employees are aware of what is expected of them. This can also help build a stronger company culture. One of the most important factors that you can consider when it comes to establishing a social environment is the establishment of a framework that allows staff members to get to know each other on a more personal level.

An intranet can help businesses identify their employees' cultural needs and provide them with the tools they need. It can also customize the communication that they need.

In earlier discussions about the digital workplace, we mentioned that it is where all the technologies that employees use to get work done reside. If the intranet is where all of the services and content that are ready to be showcased are located, then the digital workplace is where all of these are created.

The use of digital tools can help you improve the efficiency of your organization by allowing you to connect with your people and provide them with the necessary information.

A digital workplace solution can help you manage all of the details of a project, from start to finish, in one place. For instance, let's say you're working on a project called *Danube*. You can easily access all of the details of the project from a single place.

The Danube workspace allows you to work with all of the project's members on various communication platforms, such as Teams, Microsoft Office, and Yammer. There are also multiple product specs, business requirements documents, and other documents that are related to the project. Having all of these documents in one place makes it easier for everyone to complete their tasks.

In a large organization, you will typically collaborate with various groups and departments to complete tasks. This type of work can be done at the team level. There are typically around two to ten people working on a daily basis, and they have a good understanding of each other's roles and how they can contribute to the team's success.

- A community level is where multiple teams work together to develop or process something on a larger scale. For instance, Sales, Marketing, and Compliance might work together to create customer-facing material for a financial institution. However, the members of these teams still have a hard time understanding each other's roles and responsibilities, which can lead to missed opportunities.

- A network level is where third parties that don't work for the organization but are involved in the company's operations can work with the various members of the organization. For instance, if a financial institution has a distribution channel that is operated by third parties, this level of understanding of who does what decreases.

It can be frightening to think about how many different levels of collaboration are taking place in an organization at any given time. For employees who have to work on different tasks at the same time, having everyone and everything in one place is very important. Having the necessary tools and resources to complete a task is also very important to ensure that the organization's operations are running smoothly. A digital workplace solution can help you get the job done efficiently.

Instead of having everyone working at the same time, a more flexible working style is created that allows people to work on their goals without having to coordinate with others. A digital workplace is the ideal platform for this style of work.

Through the use of digital workplace tools, organizations can monitor the activities of their employees and make critical decisions based on the data collected. This data can then be used to improve performance and make informed decisions. In addition to being able to analyze and measure the effectiveness of their operations, digital workplace data can also be used to visualize how people are using it.

The differences between an intranet and a digital workplace are communication and collaboration issues. An intranet allows the audience to interact with the actors and producers in real-time, while a digital workplace allows them to see what the show's final product all is about.

The digital workplace is where everyone works together to create the show's final product. Table 4-1 shows a summary of differences between digital workplaces and intranets.

Table 4-1. *Differences Between Intranets and Digital Workplaces*

	Intranet	Digital Workplace
Objective	Source of employee- and organization-specific information	Building relationships, social networking, collaboration, works like a network
Functionality	One-way communication with the exception of the feedback feature	Employee-to-employee communication with user-generated information
Collaboration	To access the intranet, workers need to switch between applications	Access is seamless in the case of M365 services such as Yammer, Teams, and Planner
Information	Generally, shared by leads, business heads, or senior management	User-generated content
Pattern	Broadcast	Broadcast as well as targeted communication in like-minded groups
Linked Applications	Links for external application	Seamless integration between applications

Conclusion

A digital platform like SharePoint communication sites should be simple so as not to overstep the functionality of the average user. This is why it should be designed to be easy to navigate and use by everyone.

A good digital workplace solution such as a communication site should be able to organize its content effectively. It should also be easy to find and maintain and should allow the owner to update and maintain its content.

A digital workplace is full of data. In order to process this data efficiently, it needs to be built with an infrastructure that can support its users and its ongoing maintenance. The term *information architecture* refers to the design of a digital workplace that enables the organization and management of its data.

Artificial Intelligence (AI) is being used in various settings in the digital realm, and it is expected to eventually elevate the tasks that people do every day. This is because of how it can automate certain repetitive and mundane tasks.

One of the most important tasks that a SharePoint communication sites can perform is to extract key information from various documents, such as legal contracts and invoices. A machine can perform this task in seconds, and at a high accuracy rate.

It's also important that businesses thoroughly review their digital experience. Due to the lack of proper technology and the increasing complexity of today's workforce, many companies are struggling to retain and attract the best talent. This is why it's important that they adopt a comprehensive digital workplace using SharePoint communication sites, which can help them attract and retain the best talent.

End User Experiences with SharePoint Communication Sites

The latest version of Microsoft's platform, known as SharePoint Online, introduces a variety of modern experiences to its users. These changes have a direct impact on the end user experience.

Although the various benefits of the modern experiences are covered in other chapters, it's important to note that there are still options available for customization.

The various experiences that are being introduced in the platform are called "modern" experiences. They can be applied at the site or tenant level, and you can modify them if you have existing customizations. If you're not satisfied with the current state of the experience, you can defer using it until the required options are available. In the section, you learn how to enable the modern experience of a communication site from a classic SharePoint site and thereby retain the same "modern" experience.

The traditional approach to using Microsoft's content management system is to structure it in a hierarchical manner. This method tends to make it hard to share information between multiple sites. For instance, if an organization has multiple HR departments that need to share information about employee pay, it would be very difficult to share this information between them.

The classic experience of Microsoft's content management system also tends to result in the duplication of files between multiple sites. This can lead to issues with over-storage usage and version control. The modern version of Microsoft's content management system, on the other hand, has a flat architecture. Each of the sites can be associated with a different hub site.

SharePoint communication sites makes it easier for people to access relevant information. The hub site architecture also allows users to see updates and other relevant content that is related to their permissions and memberships. This feature can be very useful to organizations, as it allows them to customize the user experiences.

The goal of the communication sites is to make it easier for users to find and navigate through their content. AI technology will perform a search based on the user's previous work activity and role. It will also show results that only contain information that the user has authorized.

One of the advanced search features that is available in the Classic experience is *metadata filtering*. This allows users to filter through the contents of a file by the metadata associated with it. This feature is very useful for organizations that have specific criteria that are related to the type of document and the department that it pertains to.

Metadata can easily be added to a file in communication sites. This feature makes it easier for users to find the files that they need quickly. It can also be useful when searching for multiple items at the same time. For instance, if users are looking for contracts that were created in 2012, they can easily find them by searching for them in the metadata.

The modern experience of the communicate sites changes the way permissions are handled. Instead of having a hierarchical structure, there are now three models for managing permissions in the site. Team sites are linked to Microsoft Teams and Microsoft 365 groups, and they follow the permissions set in these solutions.

A communication site is a type of website that is designed to allow people to share information and internal communications. It has a traditional hierarchy structure. The owners, members, and visitors can add, edit, and publish content. The new approach makes it easier to manage permissions for multiple Microsoft applications, such as Microsoft 365 and communication sites.

One of the biggest differences between the modern and classic experiences is their appearance. While the former was designed to provide a simple and effective way to manage documents and intranets, the latter has become dated. There are only a few design themes available, and they lack the flexibility to be customized. Also, the templates aren't designed for mobile devices, which can be a major issue for on-the-go users.

With the release of the latest version of Microsoft's platform, known as the SharePoint Modern Experience, the appearance of the site has become more attractive. It is designed to be used as an external-facing solution for managing documents (see Figure 4-2).

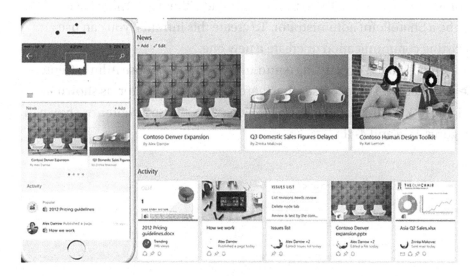

Figure 4-2. *New branding and design experience in communication sites*

To summarize, Modern Experience is the new end user experience of using communication sites. It can translated to classic sites as well.

Unfortunately, upgrading from the old version of Microsoft's platform to the modern one is not as straightforward as it should be.

In order to create a new information hierarchy in your existing site, you need to develop a strategy. You also need to take advantage of the various design options that are available with the new Microsoft Windows 10 Themes.

If your organization is planning on migrating to the modern version, or if it's planning on overhauling an existing instance, it's best to take advantage of the features that are available in the modern version and create new sites using communication sites.

Creating Intranets Using SharePoint Communication Sites

In this hands-on section, you learn how to create an intranet using communication sites. To do this, you should either have Global access or be a SharePoint administrator. To create this intranet, you can use an existing communication or create a new one.

Step 1: To use an existing communication site, choose Admin Centers ➤ SharePoint. This accesses the SharePoint Admin Center, as shown in Figure 4-3, where the active sites are located. Choose a center, as shown in Figures 4-4a and 4-4b.

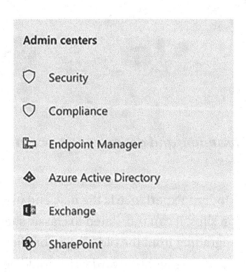

Figure 4-3. *Access SharePoint Admin Center*

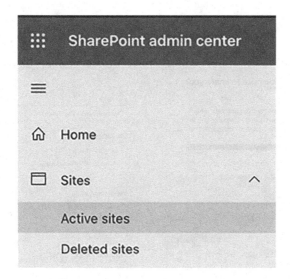

Figure 4-4a. *Choose an active site*

Figure 4-4b. *Choose an active site*

Step 2: To create a new communication site, go to the site settings and click Create a Site Page. From there, choose Communication Site, which will show the screen shown in Figure 4-5.

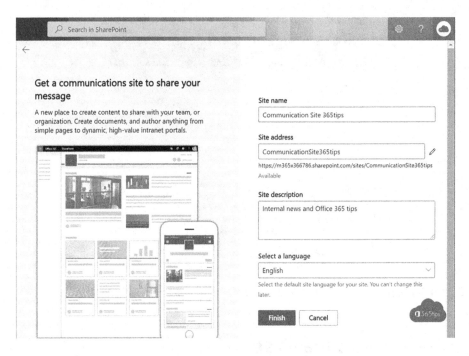

Figure 4-5. *Create a communication site*

Step 3: Enter a site name, address, owner, and preferred language. In the Advanced Settings section, you can set various additional settings for the site, such as the time zone, sensitivity, and a description. After you're satisfied with your settings, click the Finish button. After you've created a new site, it will automatically appear in the list of active sites in the Admin Center, as shown in Figure 4-6. You can choose the new site's URL from the General tab.

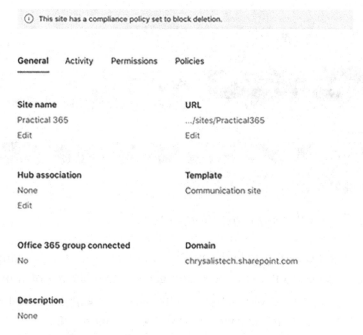

Figure 4-6. *Newly created site*

The new site is blank, and you need to design it using webparts and customization (see Figure 4-7).

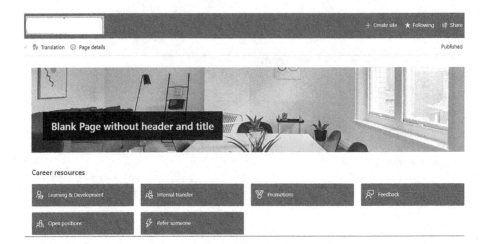

Figure 4-7. *Blank communication site*

Step 4: After creating a blank canvas, you're ready to start working on the landing page. You'll make some changes to it to make it look more like an intranet page. To customize the look of this landing page, go to the top-right corner and click the cog wheel, as shown in Figure 4-8.

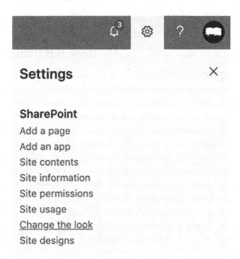

Figure 4-8. *Options for customization*

Step 5: Click Change the Look. You will then see the options to design new communication sites shown in Figure 4-9.

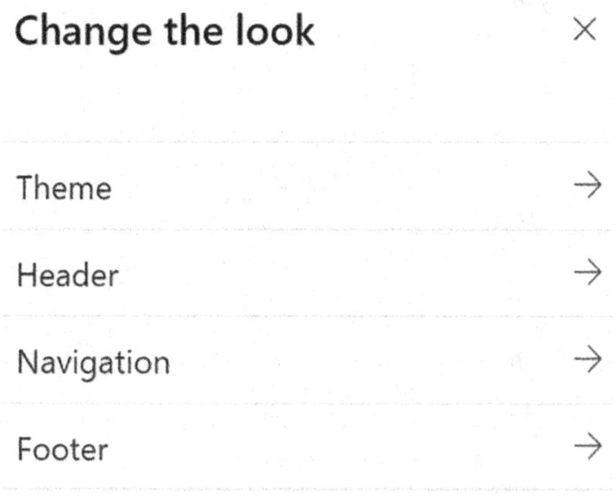

Change the look   ×

Theme	→
Header	→
Navigation	→
Footer	→

Figure 4-9. *Options to change the look and feel of the site*

Under Theme, you can choose corporate branded colors and themes. Under header, you will find options for Layout and Background themes, as shown in Figure 4-10.

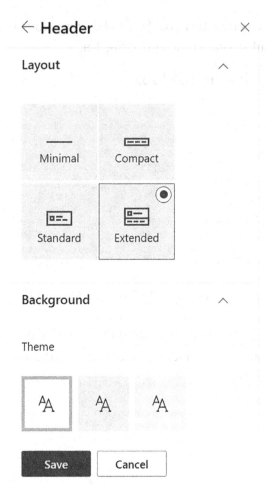

Figure 4-10. *Change the page header*

Step 6: Choose navigation, as shown in Figure 4-11.

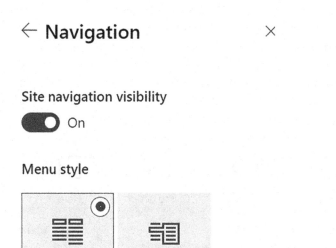

Figure 4-11. *Set up page navigation*

Step 7: Finally, edit the page to access all the webparts, as shown in Figure 4-12. You can use them to design your visually appealing intranet.

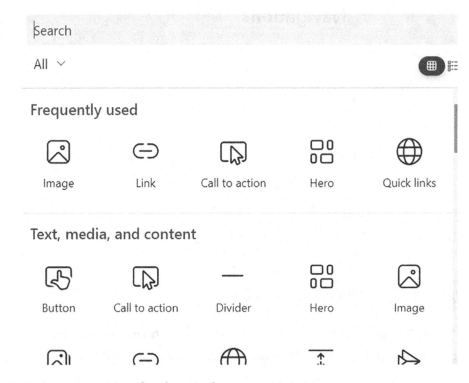

Figure 4-12. *List of webparts for customization*

Summary

In this chapter, you learned what about intranets and digital workplaces, including the differences between them and how you can use both together for best results. The next chapter explores information management and governance, how communication sites play an important role in managing information, and labeling records in communication sites.

CHAPTER 5

Information Management Compliance and Governance Using SharePoint Communication Sites

Information management (IM) involves managing an organization's various processes and systems related to the acquisition, storage, and use of information. This process is carried out through a continuous cycle of activities. The six phases of IM include identifying information needs, analyzing and interpreting information, organizing information, disseminating information, accessing information, and storing information. With the right information management and governance solutions, companies can meet their regulatory and legal requirements. They can also improve the quality of their data and ensure that they are

© Charles David Waghmare 2023

C. D. Waghmare, *Beginning SharePoint Communication Sites*,
https://doi.org/10.1007/978-1-4842-8960-0_5

compliant with the latest data privacy and security standards. This chapter focuses on aspects such as what information management is and why governance is necessary, the IM lifecycle, performing IM compliance in SharePoint communication sites, labeling records in SharePoint communication sites, decommissioning and deactivating SharePoint communication sites, and managing metadata for effective IM.

What Is Information Management and Why Is Governance Necessary?

Information is a vital part of any business operation, and it is often used to make critical decisions and improve performance. The exchange of information is very important to the success of a company. Employees benefit from having the necessary knowledge and skills to use information.

The exchange and use of information can also have risks and obligations. Misleading or inappropriate communications can lead to various legal and compliance issues.

If an organization is careless or inappropriate when it comes to the exchange of information, this can cause various issues such as reputational damage, fines, and loss of competitiveness. This can also affect the actions of its employees. In addition, poorly worded and poorly communicated information can be used against an organization in regulatory investigations or litigation.

To minimize the risk of unauthorized access and use of information, an organization should regularly review its policies and procedures. It should also ensure that it has the necessary legal and contractual requirements to protect the information it collects. Another issue that can affect the exchange of information is the sharing of information with joint ventures, which are not controlled by the company.

Information technology is also subject to various regulations and laws concerning its use and location. When it is used to process or store information, it should be taken seriously to ensure that the confidentiality, availability, and integrity of the data are protected. Having the necessary measures in place to protect information is very important to ensure that the company's operations are conducted in a secure manner.

The Information Governance Program

The concept of good governance is more than just policies and procedures. It involves having the support of various management and staff members, as well as the necessary resources to ensure that the organization's operations are conducted in the proper manner. This can be done through the establishment of a strong accountability framework at every level.

This section identifies the roles that are required to support the development and implementation of effective governance structures. These roles do not necessarily have job titles or descriptions. They may be held by multiple individuals or groups.

These roles are not limited to a particular process or repository. They also cover the governance of other information objects and other data structures within the organization.

The *program owner* is the person responsible for overseeing the implementation of the organization's programs and policies. They are also accountable to the senior management and board members for the success of the program. The owner of the organization will also work with the program steering committee and project sponsors to identify the necessary projects to further the program. The program owner is also responsible for developing and implementing the program's business case. There are various ways that an ERM (Enterprise Risk Management) program can be developed and implemented, and each of these requires its own set of policies and procedures. This can be done through the establishment of a variety of technical architectures and roles. For most organizations, the program owner is also responsible for overseeing the development and implementation of the organization's governance and compliance policies.

The *business unit manager* is responsible for the various departments and agencies within the organization. In order to effectively communicate the benefits of information management to the members of the business unit, the manager must make sure that the employees are aware of the program's goals. The first step in implementing information management is to create a business case that explains the benefits of the program. The manager of a certain business unit is responsible for ensuring that its employees are following the program's requirements. This means that the organization has to have a plan in place to address any potential issues that might arise as the program continues. The goal of the program is to make sure that all staff members are trained on the various components of the program, such as policies and procedures. This can be done through the development of training programs by either the HR department or by a third party. It's important that these are delivered regularly and that staff members are given refresher training.

The *information technology (IT) department* is a vital part of the governance effort. It can be described as either a centralized or decentralized staff, or it can be outsourced. The department is responsible for the installation, configuration, and maintenance of the systems that make up an information management system. Aside from the applications that create records and documents, these systems also include other related applications such as those for archiving and managing information. IT must ensure that the appropriate solutions are in place and can fit seamlessly into the overall architecture of the organization. Some applications, such as those that use Oracle databases for example, might not work well with an organization's existing infrastructure. This is because the company uses a Microsoft SQL Server-based architecture.

One of the most critical functions of an information management system is the *records management* function, which is responsible for creating and managing classification structures for various types of documents. This process can be used within an IM program to create and reuse these structures. For instance, by having a repository that stores information in the users' inboxes, IT can easily integrate the productivity suite with an existing IM system. The records management department is responsible for analyzing the various requirements of an organization when it comes to keeping and managing its records. It then provides recommendations on how to comply with these requirements. This department also develops policies and procedures that will help the organization manage its records. Records management should also regularly review the environment of an information management system to ensure that it supports the retention requirements. This can be done through the assessment of the various processes and technologies used within the system.

The *legal function* is a vital part of the governance of the IM program. It is responsible for overseeing the various requirements of the program, such as the production of information and the enforcement of legal holds. The legal function is also likely to receive notices of potential legal actions and other requirements. The legal function is responsible for conducting the discovery process in the event that it is required. This process involves identifying and retrieving relevant information, de-duping of that information, reviewing and protecting the information, and production of the information to the appropriate parties. Records management generally drafts policies and procedures related to the production of information. However, it is generally legal for senior management to sign off on these procedures and policies, which clears the way for their implementation.

In addition to these main roles and structures discussed, there are other roles and structures that can also help improve the effectiveness of an information governance project:

- The steering committee

- One or more centers of excellence (CoE)

- One or more communities of practice (CoP)

- Coordinators

The Steering Committee

An effective steering committee for an initiative can provide an advisory and assurance framework for the project. Usually, the committee is composed of senior managers from the program. They have the authority to make decisions regarding the project's direction.

The goal of the steering committee is to ensure that the senior managers are involved in the project's success. It also provides them with the necessary guidance and resources to make informed decisions. The owner of the project can also escalate issues that are beyond the committee's scope. This can be done through the program owner, who can then escalate the issues to other senior management. Having multiple steering committees can help an organization manage its various projects.

One or More Centers of Excellence (CoE)

A center of excellence is a governance structure that provides leadership and guidance on a particular technology or process. It can also serve as a repository of knowledge on that specific topic. Usually, these types of bodies are composed of experts on that particular field. They are typically full-time or significant-sized governing bodies. Centers of excellence can offer various benefits to an organization.

Through a center of excellence, an organization can also evaluate new practices, standards, and technologies. This can help it develop a process or technology that will help improve its operations. For instance, a center of excellence can help an organization define what is acceptable in its Microsoft SharePoint environment.

Experts in a particular field are usually members of centers of excellence. They can also serve as internal consultants for a particular topic. They can develop and deliver training and reference materials that address that specific issue. They can also identify appropriate metrics and recommendations for improvement.

One or More Communities of Practice (CoP)

A community of practice, similar to a center of excellence, is focused
on sharing knowledge. Unlike other types of communities, it tends to
be more organic as it grows. People tend to join and participate in these
groups because they want to be part of them, not because they are part of
their job descriptions. A community of practice is a type of organization
that depends on the members' interest and the availability of support. It
generally lasts for as long as it is useful and provides value to its members.
Similar to CoEs, communities of practice allow practitioners to share
knowledge and improve their skills. They also often include horror stories
and lessons learned.

While communities of practice can help individuals improve their
organizational performance, they can also be used to teach others. In 2001,
Storck and Lesser explained that these types of communities can help
improve the performance of organizations by sharing experiences and
learning from others. They noted that communities of practice can help
employees develop their skills and improve their performance by reducing
the learning curve. They can also help them respond faster to customer
inquiries and improve the quality of their products and services.

One of the main advantages of communities of practice is that they can
help identify areas of concern that should be addressed by the center of
excellence. For instance, if an organization has a local AIIM (Association
for Intelligent Information Management) chapter, its members can
participate in its community of practice. Although it is not required to join,
participants can gain significant benefits from participating in the group.
They can also share their own experiences and learn from others.

Coordinators

The last group of people to consider involves individuals who are experts
in their field. These include engineers, salespeople, and clerks, as well
as IT staff and HR personnel. They have also been trained in the use
of information governance processes such as e-discovery and records
management. These individuals act as liaisons between the various work
processes of their departments and the information governance program.

These individuals are usually tasked with raising issues related to the
use of information governance processes within their departments. They
then work with the records team to distribute information to their area.
These roles, which may be called advisors, coordinators, or liaisons, are
very important to the success of an information management initiative.

These individuals can provide first-line support to their colleagues
on various issues related to the use of information governance processes.
They can also help them locate and store information. They are often
part of the team that carries out information inventory and transfer or
destruction tasks.

Finally, putting all together, the governance model looks like Figure 5-1.

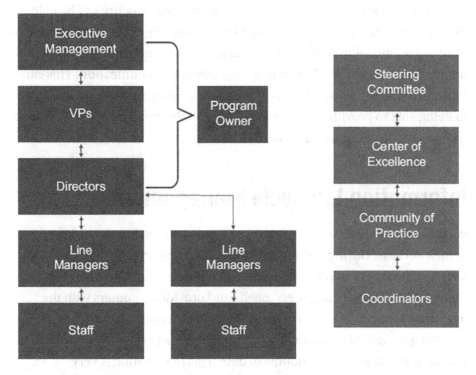

Figure 5-1. *The governance model*

Although the various governance structures that are used to manage
information governance are beneficial, there is a certain amount that
should be prioritized. One of the most important factors that can be
considered is the establishment of a steering committee. This group will
help resolve conflicts among the competing priorities and ensure that the
information governance process is delivered effectively.

The most important aspect of information governance is having a
culture that supports continuous improvement. However, coordinators can
also help improve the effectiveness of the process by developing effective
communities of practice. They should not force people to participate, and
they should provide resources such as a meeting room, but they should
work more naturally.

One of the most important factors that information governance coordinators should consider is having the necessary maturity to be able to set and enforce standards. This can be done through the establishment of strong relationships with management. Another important aspect of information governance is having the necessary communication. This can be done through the use of effective communication methods. In addition to being able to provide a variety of effective tools, the communication should also be tailored to the needs of the organization.

Information Lifecycle Management

Big and small businesses are realizing that information is now the key to their success. Having the necessary tools and resources to collect and analyze data is very important for them to be successful. This allows them to identify their customers' needs and provide customers with the necessary services. They can also reach out to potential customers by analyzing the data they collect. Over the years, many businesses have collected and stored vast amounts of data. This information is very important to their operations and profitability, and it needs to be handled properly to ensure that it is not outdated. A company collects, stores, and classifies data and then automatically removes it when it becomes obsolete.

Information lifecycle management is a vital part of any company's operations, as it allows them to continuously manage their data throughout its lifecycle. This type of solution can help them improve the performance of their applications and reduce their infrastructure costs. With the right information lifecycle management solution, organizations can improve their infrastructure and reduce their costs. It can also help them establish a control framework for their data. According to industry experts, a lot of the data that organizations rely on is not current. Having the necessary tools and resources to manage their data is very important for them to be successful.

This type of solution can help prevent companies from running out of resources when it comes to managing their data. It can also help them keep track of all of their data's activities and ensure that it is always in compliance with regulations.

Overview of Information Management Lifecyle

The process of managing the information lifecycle is a process that involves overseeing the creation, maintenance, and disposition of data. It helps organizations reduce their costs and improve their efficiency by minimizing the risks associated with the data. This type of management also helps organizations align their requirements with the policies and procedures of their data.

Throughout the lifecycle of a company's information, it is important that it is managed properly. The information lifecycle management process begins when an organization receives or creates a record. It then covers various aspects of the data's usage, maintenance, and storage. Once the information is complete, it is either destroyed or stored in accordance with the established retention schedule. This type of management is also beneficial for protecting the privacy and security of the information.

Best practices for information lifecycle management include strategies to improve the quality of data, utility optimization, and safety.

Information lifecycle management (ILM) is a key component of any organization's business strategy to meet the increasing demand for information. It should be integrated into their various processes and applications to ensure that they are able to manage their growing data.

In addition to being central to their operations, businesses should also implement a policy-based approach to manage their information assets. This ensures that they have the necessary tools and resources to manage their growing data. The ILM should also be designed to allocate the appropriate resources based on the needs of the organization. It should consider the various types of storage platforms and operating systems that are available to the organization.

Information Lifecycle Management Process

Before a company or organization can start its operations, it must
thoroughly research and collect information. This process involves
gathering data about its customers and competitors, as well as determining
the optimal strategy for its products and services. When a company starts
its operations, it collects and creates information that it uses to improve its
processes and procedures. This information is then stored and managed
in a way that it can be retrieved whenever required. As the company or
organization ages, it eventually stops archiving and deleting old data. It
also secures the data to prevent unauthorized individuals from accessing
it. This process ensures that the organization uses the information
collected for its operations and decisions.

The information lifecycle management policy is actually a set of
policies designed to drive the various processes of an organization's
information management system. These policies are usually aligned with
the business goals and drivers of the company.

There are many challenges that businesses face when it comes to
managing their data, and they need to consider the various goals that will
help them achieve their goals. The goal of ILM is to provide a framework
that will allow them to efficiently manage their data.

- **Data security and confidentiality:** Due to the
  immense amount of data that's collected and stored
  in the world, it's very important that organizations
  take the necessary steps to protect their data. This is
  because it's becoming the new currency in the digital
  world. Besides protecting their own data, it's also
  important that organizations protect their external
  users from unauthorized access.

- **Availability:** It's also important that organizations have the necessary tools and resources to ensure that their data is readily available when needed. This can help prevent costly errors and disruptions in their operations. Lack of availability can lead to cascading failures of processes that rely on previous information.

- **Integrity:** Due to the nature of data, it's often subject to multiple revisions and changes during every instance of use. This is why it's important that organizations have the necessary tools and resources to ensure that their data is readily available when needed. In addition to protecting their own data, it's also important that they implement the necessary technologies to ensure that their users are able to access the correct information.

Information Lifecycle Management Strategy

A comprehensive ILM strategy can help businesses manage their data and protect their storage media. It can also help them determine how they should treat their data and help them leverage their storage media's tiers. Without a backup in place, businesses can't access or make corrections to their data, applications, or information. This is why it's important that they have an information lifecycle management strategy that coordinates the various lifecycles of their data.

Data is still active from a reading perspective even if it's been continuously produced and stored in different locations. Understanding this allows businesses to improve their understanding of how to protect their data in the future. For instance, by protecting static data frequently, they can prevent it from being lost or damaged. With the right ILM strategy, businesses can unlock value and lower their costs by reducing complexity and improving their data management. This can be done by reviewing their existing information management and implementing new strategies.

Phases of Information Lifecycle Management

There are various phases in the information lifecycle management process for different industries. It is possible to classify these phases into different groups depending on their complexity.

Data Collection

Online and offline sources of data are often used by businesses to collect information about their customers. Social media networks and the Internet are some of the most common sources of free and paid data. However, some companies provide more accurate information based on their customers' requirements.

Data Creation

As a company begins its operations, it starts gathering and storing information on a large scale. This data is then used to improve its operations and provide its customers with better service.

Data Classification

Before storing any data, the business will classify it to make it easier to access and retrieve. This process helps companies store and retrieve information more efficiently. Large organizations store data in databases that have many processing facilities, which makes it more valuable. They classify it into various tiers to ensure that the information is kept in its proper place.

Data Archiving

Due to the complexity of the data collected and stored, it can be hard to
keep track of all of it. This is why it is important that the company regularly
archives and documents the data to make it available to its customers
whenever they need it.

Data Security

Regardless of whether it is archived or real-time, businesses should
ensure that their data is protected from various threats. This is because the
increasing number of attacks and breaches on companies' networks has
made it important for them to take measures to protect their data.

Data Disposal

Besides keeping track of all of its data, businesses should also ensure
that their data is properly disposed of when it's no longer needed. This is
because the increasing number of threats and breaches on companies'
networks has made it important for them to take measures to properly
remove or archive unneeded data.

Data Assignment

Over time, data becomes obsolete due to various factors such as changing
policies, implementing new procedures, or adopting a better strategy.
Unfortunately, it can be very costly to maintain and recover outdated data.
Having a periodic information assessment is also important to ensure that
the company's data is still in its proper place.

Having an information assessment is also important to ensure that the
company's data is still in its proper place. This process can help them make

better decisions and improve their operations. One of the most common
ways businesses can store and retrieve data is by creating and storing
bulk data.

Records Management in SharePoint Communication Sites

Organizations of all types need a records-management solution that
can help them manage their legal obligations and business-critical
records. Microsoft Purview provides a comprehensive solution that helps
organizations comply with regulations and improve their efficiency.
Records management can help an organization maintain its compliance
with regulations while reducing its risk of errors and omissions.

Although Microsoft's Purview compliance portal can help you
create and manage retention labels, it does not provide the necessary
management capabilities for managing them. With the help of File Plan
from Records Management, you can create and manage these labels from
a spreadsheet. You can also export the information from these labels to
other applications for offline collaboration.

You can now see more information about the various types of retention
labels in one view by clicking the View Details button. File Plan descriptors
support optional and additional information for each label. Even if the
content doesn't appear as a record in the File Plan, it can still be used for
all labels.

To access File Plan from the Records Management section of
Microsoft's Purview compliance platform, you must have a certain admin
role. You can also access it from the File Plan menu in the Solutions
section, as shown in Figure 5-2.

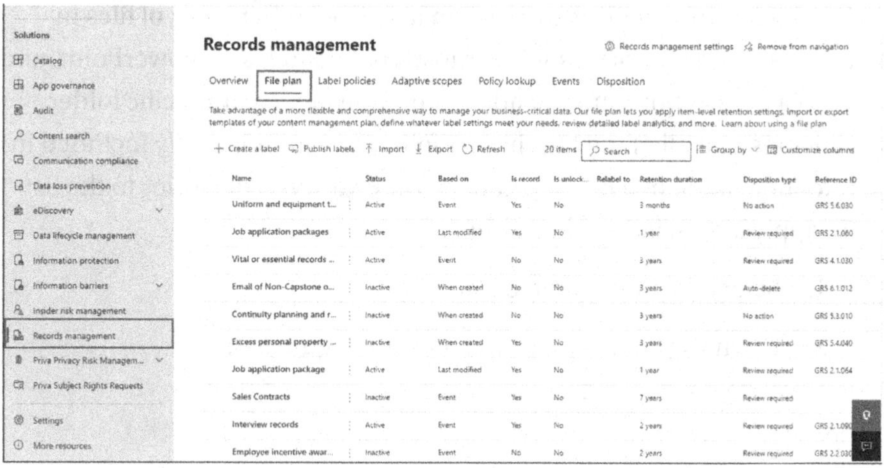

Figure 5-2. *File Plan console*

If the navigation pane doesn't show the Records Management section, click the Show All button. If you've previously created retention labels in the Data Lifecycle Management section of Microsoft's Purview compliance platform, they will automatically appear in File Plan. If you're still using the old version of the software, you can also add new retention labels to File Plan if they don't have to be marked as a record.

On the File Plan page, you can see all of your retention labels' settings and status. You can also export the information from these labels to other applications to allow offline reviews.

Applying Labels in SharePoint Online

You can easily apply retention labels to files in Microsoft 365 platform, such as in the form of folders or individual files. The labels have been customized according to your organization's requirements. If you have any questions about which one to apply, contact your IT department or help desk.

In addition to specific files, you can also label other types of files in Microsoft's cloud platform, such as those created in Excel, PowerPoint, and Word. In a library, you can also add a retention label to a specific folder. This ensures that all of the files in that folder are automatically included in the retention label. In a list, you can also add various categories to the list.

To apply labels, follow these steps:

1. Select the item or attachment.

2. Open the details pane, as shown in Figure 5-3.

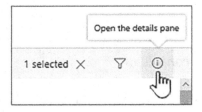

Figure 5-3. *Open the details pane*

3. Choose a label and apply it, as shown in Figure 5-4.

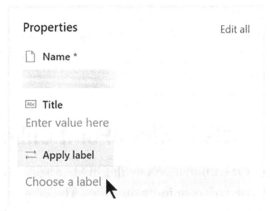

Figure 5-4. *Apply a label*

4. Select the label and save. The file is then labelled as
    a record using this File Plan.

To set a default label, follow these steps:

1. Open the Document Library and click the Settings
    icon at the top-right side of the window. On the next
    page, choose the settings icon for the library or list.

2. Under the Management and Permissions section,
    click the Apply Label button. On the next page, you
    can select the drop-down box to apply the label that
    you want to use.

3. The label you select will automatically be applied to
    all new files that are added to the Document Library.
    You can also apply the label to all existing files in the
    library by selecting Apply Label to all items.

In addition to being able to view the contents of a library in a single
view, you can also create a view that shows the various retention labels that
are associated with each item in the library. This method can be useful if
you want to see which items are records and which ones are not. However,
you can't filter the view by the item's name.

The Retention Label column can be easily made visible in the list
view by clicking the down arrow icon in the top-right corner, as shown in
Figure 5-5. You can also expand the details of the column by selecting the
chevron icon. In the Edit View pane, select the check box for Retention
Label, as shown in Figure 5-6.

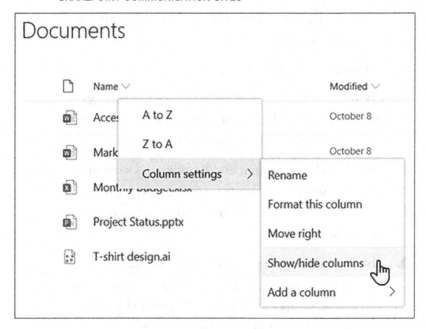

Figure 5-5. *View with retention labels*

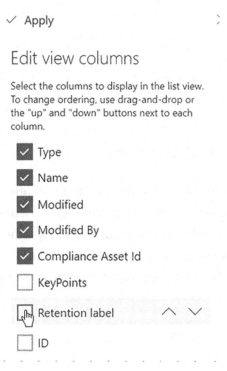

Figure 5-6. *View Retention Label column*

Some retention labels allow users to lock an item so that it can be kept
as a record that is required to be preserved. This is useful for certain types
of records, such as contracts. However, it can also be used to unlock an
item so that it can be updated or revised. In the list or library, choose the
item you want to unlock. You can also open the details pane, as shown in
Figure 5-7.

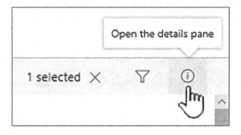

Figure 5-7. *Open the details pane*

In the details pane, under the Record Status, choose the lock. A toggle
control appears beside the name of the setting. You can then switch
from locked to unlocked by clicking the toggle. After the item has been
unlocked, you can then edit it. Toggling the Record Status back to its
original state will allow you to continue with the process, as shown in
Figure 5-8.

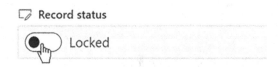

Figure 5-8. *Unlocking records*

Decommissioning and Deactivating SharePoint Communication Sites

When SharePoint sites are unused for lack of activity, it is best to
decommission them in order to save space on the Microsoft 365 platform.
If the site owners need some time before decommissioning, it is best to
make such sites read-only or deactivate them.

Before decommissioning sites, they are checked for content and
records. If there is relevant content, it is moved to another repository. For

regulatory reasons, records are not actually deleted, but are moved to separate SharePoint sites.

As a global administrator or administrator in Microsoft 365, you can remove a site from the system for up to 93 days. This process automatically deletes everything that's in it, including the files, documents, and lists that are stored in it. Other subsites and their contents are also deleted. Before you remove a site, you should notify its administrators and subsite owners. This will allow them to move their data to another location.

You can also remove both modern and classic sites through the Admin Center of Microsoft 365. Global administrators can now remove sites that belong to groups within the company. Deleting these sites will remove all of the resources of the group, including the calendars and the Outlook email.

In the Admin Center of Microsoft 365, go to the Active Sites section and sign in with your account. In the left column, click the button that says Select a Site. You can also confirm or select Delete. See Figure 5-9 for details.

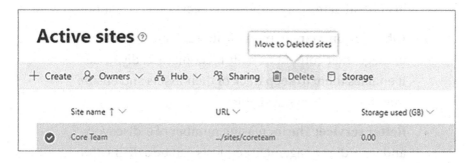

Figure 5-9. *Deleting a site*

Note   If you want to remove a site from the new Admin Center of Microsoft 365, you can do so by unregistering it from the list of hub sites or by deleting it based on its type.

Benefits of Information Lifecycle Management

Information lifecycle management is a vital part of any organization's strategy to succeed in today's competitive environment. It can help boost customer service, improve efficiency, and manage risk.

The implementation of information lifecycle management can transform the way businesses manage their data. It can help them reduce the complexity of their information technology infrastructures and improve their performance. It can also help them develop new business capabilities by reducing the amount of information that they store and manage. Consider these benefits:

- **Limited risks:** ILM helps organizations reduce the amount of non-essential information that they store and manage. It eliminates the risk of data loss and helps them find and manage their data more easily. By knowing where to find all of the information that's stored in their data, businesses can reduce the likelihood of missing important pieces of information.

- **Information management:** With ILM, businesses can manage their content from its creation to its disposal. It enables them to keep track of their assets and ensure that they are always available.

- **Better service:** The increasing number of e-discovery and records management requests can be a distraction for both the legal and IT departments. By reducing the number of these requests, both parties can focus on their core business.

- **Saved costs:** With the help of ILM, businesses can reduce their e-discovery and legal hold costs. They can also improve their chances of finding important information quickly. One of the most important factors that businesses consider when it comes to reducing their e-discovery costs is the reduction of digital debris.

- **Faster access:** Categorizing the data collected, stored, or created under ILM can speed up access to the information.

- **Smart governance:** It can also introduce management controls that will benefit the organization. ILM can help improve the information management of all businesses.

Regardless of whether a company is in the financial services, insurance, or online retailers, information lifecycle management is the same. This process involves continuously monitoring and improving the information that's collected and stored.

Before a company starts its information lifecycle management, it needs to determine its feasibility. This process then involves collecting and storing data for various reasons. They then use tools such as business intelligence to analyze and improve their processes.

Due to the importance of information, businesses need to take the necessary steps to protect their data. This can be done through the use of secure storage and records management. They can also reduce the amount of data they store by using records management to archive and store it.

The more innovative companies that implement information lifecycle management are able to benefit from it.

Managing Metadata for Effective IM

Once the content has been captured or created by an organization, you need to extract information from it to provide context. This section talks about how to create and develop metadata and taxonomies. You'll also learn how to automate the process of creating these two types of documents. In the end, the section covers how to use powerful data extraction and recognition technologies to create effective and meaningful metadata.

Machine learning and analytics tools can help improve the efficiency of information management. They can also help users find the information they need to perform their jobs. In addition, this section covers how to create search capabilities that are designed to help users find the information they need.

Information in Context

The information domain is the gateway to the organization's goals and objectives. It needs to be used in a way that supports the users while not burdening them. This is why it's important that you take advantage of the latest analytics and recognition technologies to automate and streamline the way you develop that context.

Although the information domain is made up of various tools, they should not be used to drive the organization's goals and objectives. Instead, they should be used to support the business's needs and improve the customer experience. One of the most important factors that organizations should consider when it comes to adopting new technologies is the ability to understand and use the data they collect.

The Benefits of Metadata

There is no single definition of metadata. Instead, there are many different definitions and descriptions of metadata that cover the same points. This is why it is important that you adopt the one that is most relevant to your organization's information management activities.

Metadata is a set of characteristics and data elements that describe the structure and content of an organization's records. According to

International Standards Organization (ISO) 15489, "Data describing records is a description of the information structure and content of a record." The U.S. Department of Defense's (DoD) 5015.2 standard provides a similar definition. This is because, similar to the ISO standard, the DOD's definition of metadata describes the data elements and the context of the data. This helps in the development of information management systems.

Metadata is often used to describe the structure and content of an organization's records. It can also help in the development of information management systems by describing the data elements and the context of the data.

Perspectives on Metadata

When entering metadata values, the process is often referred to as "indexing." This is a form of confirmation that an item has been captured, and it's easier to say, "have you checked those documents" rather than "have you entered the metadata for them yet?"

According to ISO 23081, metadata can support various needs. This is because different perspectives and views on metadata can exist. There are two main perspectives on metadata: the business perspective and the user view. The former focuses on the ability to retrieve and interpret content, while the latter is on the security and privacy considerations. The latter is on the governance side, which includes topics such as lifecycle management and security.

The Business Value of Metadata

Metadata is a vital part of any organization's content management system, as it determines the alignment of various business goals and objectives. It can also be used to organize content by identifying its dates and events. For instance, it can be used to monitor the distribution of a document's records.

Metadata can also be used to capture the rating of content by users, for example, if the content is valuable or outdated. It is very important that the metadata is captured at the same time the content is being created and stored. If the content is not captured at the same time, it will create a collection of documents that is difficult to retrieve and manage. This is why it is very useful to have a search and retrieval mechanism.

Metadata can also provide users with greater precision when it comes to searching and retrieving information. It can be used to target specific fields in a document, such as the author, subject, and date. This is because metadata can help improve the efficiency of the content management system. It can additionally help improve the way the information is accessed and managed by business processes.

If the date of the receipt of a document is not captured as a metadata value, it will not allow the documents to be reviewed in the correct order. This issue can prevent the organization from achieving its goals and objectives.

Metadata can be used to process documents in batches, which is beneficial for organizations as it allows them to retrieve and manage multiple pieces of information at the same time. For instance, if an organization has multiple projects going on, tracking the status of each project can help in batch processing. This process can also lead to the creation of expert databases of information.

Metadata can also be used to integrate different applications. For instance, if an organization has multiple projects going on, tracking the status of each project can help in batch processing. Even though the content is stored in different systems, it can be linked through common values and properties. This can help improve the efficiency of the organization's information management system.

One of the most important factors that businesses consider when it comes to implementing business intelligence is the ability to analyze the data collected by various processes. For instance, if an organization has multiple projects going on, tracking the status of each project can help in batch processing. One of the most useful features of this process is the ability to capture the characteristics of the documents, such as the customer IDs and the type of invoice.

One of the most important factors that businesses consider when it comes to implementing business intelligence is the ability to analyze the data collected by various processes. For instance, if an organization has multiple projects going on, tracking the status of each project can help in batch processing. Metadata can also be used to enhance knowledge management by identifying experts and referring to their profiles.

The Metadata Strategy

Metadata is a type of data that is used to store and retrieve information. It is used in various systems to store and retrieve data. Unfortunately, in too many organizations, the different approaches and structures to data management make it hard to find and manage. For instance, in one system, an employee's name is listed as "first name" and "last name," while in another, it is "last name (comma)".

To avoid this, an organization should develop a comprehensive metadata strategy. This strategy will help identify and define the various ways that metadata will be used to store and retrieve information, and it will also improve the ability to manage its content. This strategy will help ensure that the data is used consistently across the organization.

Guidelines to Determining Metadata

Metadata design is a process that an organization should adopt in order to ensure that its documents are stored and accessed in a way that is easy to find and retrieve. However, before implementing this strategy, it's important to first identify the various types of content that are needed to make the documents work. This can be done by determining what kinds of documents are available to users and how they are retrieved.

When you first start working with a client, you may use their
identification number to retrieve a document, but you prefer to use their
name once you have become familiar with them.

Before implementing this strategy, it's important that the organization
has an ideal scenario in place. This can be achieved by creating a file
system that is designed to work seamlessly with the various types of
documents that are stored in it.

When creating content, it's important to think about the things that
you created instead of the things that will be retrieved in the future. This
ensures that both the client and the document are well-thought-out before
any costly changes are made.

Tasks for Determining Metadata

Metadata and documents that are shared among departments or groups
should be consistent across all of them. For instance, a record that is used
in payroll may be shared with accounting or human resources, but each
department has its own unique needs when it comes to retrieving that
record. It's important to make sure that all possible exceptions are covered
in order to maximize the value of the column.

The time it takes to enter metadata values should be monitored. If
it's too long, your users might try to circumvent the entry process, or they
might store the documents in other locations. If they don't want to fill in
the data, consider reducing the amount of metadata that you need to have
in order to ensure that the documents are stored in the correct format.

Before you start working on implementing a new project, it's important
that you thoroughly analyze the existing filing structures. This will help you
identify the types of metadata that you need to have in order to improve
the efficiency of your operations. You should also create an enterprise data
dictionary, which is designed to help you store and retrieve data in the
correct format.

Mandatory vs. Optional Metadata

There are a variety of options when it comes to mandatory elements in the
form of entries, and the choice between having too many or too few can
be very challenging. For instance, users may find it tedious to enter their
values, while others may enter almost nothing about the item. However,
some entries can be conditional, which is allowed under certain standards.
This function would be useful for creating a list of mandatory entries for an
item of correspondence, such as a letter. However, it would not be relevant
for a project schedule.

The Location element might be mandatory for certain physical objects,
such as books or DVDs, but it might not be relevant for digital records. This
is because records management staff members often want to have as much
metadata as possible in order to achieve a rich repository. This is typically
at odds with the community, as many users don't want to spend the time
and effort required to enter it.

This section talks about the various steps involved in creating a list of
mandatory entries. You will also learn how to use automation techniques
to improve the efficiency of the process.

The Metadata Model

A field should also be formatted with a variety of values, such as date,
currency, and number. This can be used to search for various ranges, such
as "all invoices over $1,000" or "all expense reports over $1,000".

Although some fields are less useful than others, if they are not
mandatory, then users will have to manually enter them. This can cause
issues with completeness and uptake.

The source of the data should also be determined. Usually, it is a
system or default field that is used to capture data. The owner or steward of
the data should have the authority to interpret and store it.

Due to the increasing number of jurisdictions that have enacted regulations related to data protection and privacy, it is also important to identify the types of fields that contain sensitive and personal information.

Metadata Standards

Metadata standards are available to help you organize and store information. Some of these include ISO 11179, Dublin Core, and ISO 23081. Having a variety of standards can help you make informed decisions when it comes to implementing automation.

Although there are many standards out there, we do not recommend using one standard for every organization. In most cases, none of them are ideal for every situation. Having the appropriate metadata model is also important to ensure that the information is stored and accessed in a way that is appropriate for the organization.

Metadata Automation

Due to the volume of information being captured and created in an organization, it is very difficult to sell manual entry, as it is not ideal. One of the elements that should be included in the strategy is automation. This is because, while it is not necessary to have specific approaches for this, it is important to address how automation can be used.

Introduction to Managed Metadata in SharePoint Communication Sites

As explained, metadata is a set of information that can be used to identify and retrieve various pieces of information, such as a book's title and author. With the help of a variety of tools, such as the Microsoft 365 platform, you can easily manage the metadata in your organization. It can be used to make it easier to find what you're looking for, and it can help you organize your data.

A *taxonomy* is a type of formal classification system that describes the terms and words that describe a certain concept. It then arranges these terms into a hierarchy.

The *folksonomy* is an informal system that evolves as people interact with each other on a website. It was originally developed as a result of popular applications such as Google Books.

A *term set* is a collection of related terms that can be used in various ways. There are two types of terms sets: local and global. The former is created within a site collection, and it can be used by users only. For instance, if you create a term set for an information column in a library or list, then the term set is considered local and can only be used by the users of that collection.

A *media library* can have a metadata column that describes the kind of media that it has. This column is only relevant to the library, and it can be used to retrieve other terms.

A global term set can be used across multiple sites that subscribe to a specific managed metadata service. For instance, an organization can create a term set that lists the names of various business units.

A term set is a single item that you associate with an item on a site that's in a collection. It can have multiple text labels, and it can also have a unique ID. If you work with a multilingual site, then the term can have labels in multiple languages.

A managed term is a type of term that's pre-defined. It can be used in a way that allows administrators to organize it into a hierarchical term set.

One of the types of terms that a user can add to an item on a site is an *enterprise keyword*. This type of term can be used in folksonomy-style tagging. When a user adds a word or phrase to an item, it can be used in the context of the term set. Usually, the term is placed in a managed term set. When a user adds a new term to an existing term set, it can be included in the context of that term set.

The term *store management tool* is a tool that can be used by people who are involved in the management of various terms in a site collection. It can be used to create and manage global and local term sets. The tool can also display all the terms that are available in its site collection.

Using the Term Store Management Tool

A global administrator or a SharePoint admin in the Microsoft 365 platform can access the term store management tool from the Admin Center. Once you open SharePoint's Admin Center, under Content Services, choose Term Store.

A term group is composed of sets of term sets that all share the same security requirements. Only members of a specific group can manage or create new term sets. Click Add Term Group, as shown in Figure 5-10, to create a term group.

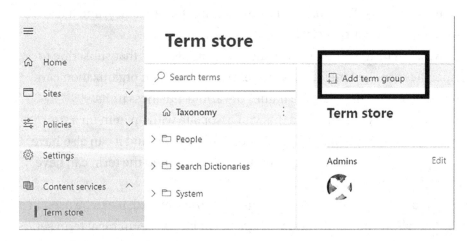

Figure 5-10. Adding a term group in the Term Store

Setting Up a New Term Set

Only the term store admin or contributor can create a term set. To create a
term set, click Add Term Set, as shown in Figure 5-11.

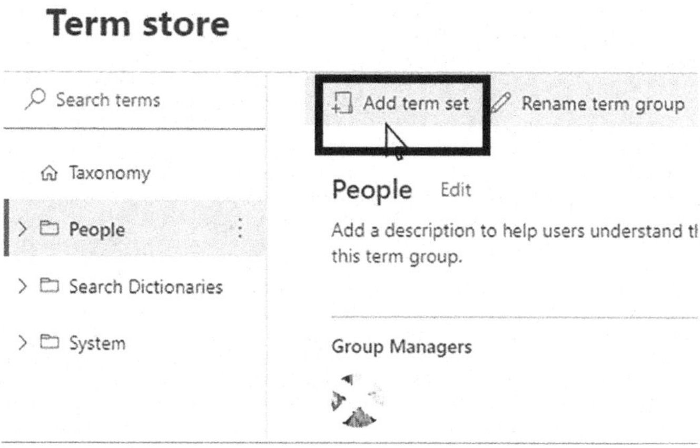

Figure 5-11.   *Creating a term set*

A term store admin can create and delete term sets and remove add/
group managers, contributors, and term store admins. The term store
admin can perform any action that's performed by a group manager or
contributor. Term store admins are assigned from the Term Store page.

The group manager can add/remove contributors. You have to be
either a term store admin or a group manager of a specific group to
add contributors to that group. All the roles can be assigned from the
SharePoint Admin Center. Under Content Services, select Term Store.

Summary

This chapter explained information management and its lifecycle
governance, records management in SharePoint communication sites,
and metadata management. The next chapter discusses integration of

SharePoint communication sites with Microsoft 365 services to explore
the various features and capabilities of Microsoft Forms, Power Apps, and
Teams. They can be integrated seamlessly into the communication sites of
your choice.

CHAPTER 6

Using SharePoint Communication Sites for Project Management

Previous chapters explored integrating SharePoint communications with Microsoft 365 services such as Forms, Power Automate, and Teams. This chapter explores the use of SharePoint Online for project management. It covers business challenges, how SharePoint communication sites can prove useful, and business benefits. You will also see how different modules in project management are managed using SharePoint communication sites. In short, the chapter explains what project management is, covers project management activities using SharePoint communication sites, includes a use case on project management, and finally discusses external sharing using SharePoint communication sites.

Upon reading this chapter, you will be able to manage and label records in SharePoint Online for project management purposes. Further, you will be able to deal with project management challenges and retrieve useful information from a SharePoint communication site page to track project status and create reports.

© Charles David Waghmare 2023

C. D. Waghmare, *Beginning SharePoint Communication Sites*,
https://doi.org/10.1007/978-1-4842-8960-0_6

Introduction to Project Management

A *project* is a temporary exercise that an organization can undertake to address a specific need. Projects can be used to create a new product or service, or they can help improve a business process. This type of project is different from how an organization typically works.

An organization's work is considered functional if it involves manufacturing something, such as trucks, on a continuous basis. This means that the same products and services are produced over and over again, and the people who perform these roles are also continuously engaged.

Project Management

A project is typically initiated by an organization for the sole purpose of improving its operations. It can be a one-off undertaking that requires a lot of resources and time, and it can be very challenging to manage due to the constraints of the project. A project team is composed of various individuals, such as end users, IT specialists, business analysts, and the project sponsor.

The concept of project management is a process that involves managing all aspects of a project in order to ensure that the resources are able to deliver the necessary output to meet the requirements of the project. This process is usually agreed upon during the project's initiation stage. Once the project begins, all team members and stakeholders will have a clear understanding of the project's methodology and expected outcomes.

A good project manager can use a formal process to manage the project, and this can be used as a reference for the project. This method can also be used to audit the project's progress.

Project Management Methodology

Projects are usually divided into three phases: the initiation, the implementation, and the closure. Each phase has multiple checkpoints that have to be met before the next phase can begin. The degree to which projects are managed depends on the size of the project and the complexity of the task. For instance, if a large project is being carried out in an organization with a lot of resources and people, a more structured approach is required. This method will allow the project to deliver the anticipated end result.

A simple project in a small organization can be done with a few checklists and a few goals. Having someone else coordinate the project is also usually all that's needed.

Initiating a Project

The initial idea for a project is usually a product or service that needs to be improved or changed. This is done through a project charter or mandate, which is a document that describes the necessary steps to start a project. The goal of the charter or mandate is to establish a clear method for presenting a project, and it should result in a business case.

After the business case has been approved, a more detailed document, known as the Project Definition Report (PD), is prepared. This document provides a comprehensive analysis of the project and its various phases. It also helps in assessing the project's viability.

This section provides a comprehensive overview of the various aspects of a project, including the scope of the project, the results of the feasibility study, and the expected duration of the project. It also identifies the key individuals and resources that will be needed to carry out the project. A project's goal is usually to achieve a certain amount of goals. They can be broken down into objectives to measure how well the project has been carried out.

Before a project can start, it must first identify the key success criteria that will determine its success or failure. These are the objectives that will be achieved even if other goals are not met. Once the project is given the go ahead, a contract document is prepared, and the project sponsor uses this document to give formal approval to the funding of the project. The initiation phase is usually completed following the contract document's approval.

Project Implementation

The implementation phase of a project involves managing and tracking the various aspects of the project. The first step in this process is to create a project plan, which describes how the project will be conducted. This is done by using the Project Definition Report, which is a summary of the project. However, a detailed project plan is required to fill in the details of the project, which is more important when the project is being run.

The project plan is a document that describes the various aspects of a project that will be carried out during the duration of the project. It is the central document that all of the team members agree on. It also provides a list of all the tasks and milestones that will be completed.

In addition to the project plan, other steps such as change control and quality control are also taken during the implementation phase. One of the most important factors that a team should consider when it comes to planning a project is the risk management process. This process involves assessing the various factors that could affect the project's success.

In addition to the project plan, a risk log is also used to record and grade the various risks that can affect the project. This document can be used to identify areas of concern and develop an action plan to minimize the risks.

Issues management is also an area that involves identifying the various concerns that the team members and other stakeholder groups have about the project. This process can be carried out through regular meetings. The project manager in quality control ensures that the products that are being produced by the team are meeting the standards set by the project.

The project manager is also responsible for monitoring the progress of the project and providing regular reports to the team members and other stakeholder groups. This process is carried out to ensure that the project is on track and that the necessary steps are being followed. As most projects do not go exactly according to plan, progress control is carried out to make sure that the plan is followed and that the appropriate actions are taken if the deviations occur.

This process can be carried out through regular checkpoints. These meetings are designed to monitor and control the activities of the project, as well as gather statistics about the team members' progress. They can also help the project manager keep track of the various tasks and milestones that will be completed.

Sometimes, projects don't go exactly according to plan. In order to ensure that the project is on track and that the necessary steps are being followed, changes are also made to the schedule.

This process can also be fully documented by the project manager in the form of change control. This process involves gathering information about the proposed changes, as well as identifying the potential impact of the changes on the project. The project manager then informs the team members and other stakeholders about the alternatives and implications of the proposed change.

The implementation phase of a project usually ends once the project has reached its goals and objectives. This stage can be carried out through the detailed success criteria in the project's definition report.

Project Manager

Aside from having the necessary knowledge about the project management methodology, a good project manager also needs to have the necessary skills and abilities to manage a project team. These include having good communication skills, being a team player, being able to negotiate, and having good interpersonal abilities.

One of the most critical factors that project managers consider when it comes to choosing and recruiting project team members is the availability of qualified individuals. This is done in a manner that is consistent with the discipline and rigor that the business requires in order to successfully carry out its projects.

Having a well-documented and adaptable methodology is also a critical element for ensuring that a project is successful. This method should be communicated to the team members during the start of the project so they have a clear understanding of what is expected of them and how it will be implemented. This will help ensure that the project is being carried out according to the requirements of the project.

Project Lifecyle

The various phases of a project are referred to as the lifecycle of living beings, and there is no universal consensus on how many phases a project should have. Understanding the lifecycle is very important to ensure that the project is completed successfully. It allows you to visualize the sequence of events in the project's development.

The typical project involves four phases: conceptualization, planning, execution, and termination. Each phase is characterized by deliverables such as a concept note, feasibility report, implementation plan, evaluation report, and resource allocation plan.

Conceptualization

The concept phase is the initial step in developing a project idea. It involves identifying the product or service that will be beneficial to the project, examining the various factors that will affect the project's success, and coming up with a strategy and a proposal that will be presented to the stakeholders. During this stage, a proposal is developed to establish the necessary details for the appraisal of the stakeholders.

Planning

The next step involves planning and implementing the project structure based on the approval and appraisal of the project. This phase also involves the preparation of the project's budget and the establishment of the project's activities. Some of the tasks that are performed in this phase include identifying the activities and their sequencing, the time frame for execution, the staffing, and the detailed project report.

Execution

The next phase of the project involves the continuous monitoring and control of the various activities of the project. This phase is focused on ensuring that the plans are being executed properly and that the project is on track. Some of the key activities that this phase involves include communicating with the stakeholders, reviewing the progress of the project, managing the quality of the work, and monitoring the cost.

Termination

The completion of the project signifies the end of the project's activities and the installation of the agreed-upon deliverables. This phase also involves the establishment of the project's follow-up and evaluation procedures.

Project Management Roles and Responsibilities

Project management roles and responsibilities include the following:

- **Board:** The board is composed of representatives from the supplier and user communities. It is chaired by the Senior Resource Officer (SRO). The board has overall responsibility for project success.

- **Accountable board member:** The board of directors of a project is composed of individuals with overall responsibility for the project. The project's senior management officer (SRO) is the key decision maker who is responsible for overseeing the project's progress and developing plans.

- **User community:** This board member is responsible for ensuring that the project products and services are delivered to the users and is accountable for their success.

- **Supplier:** This board member is also responsible for ensuring that the project's products and services are of high quality.

- **Project manager:** The project's prime minister is also responsible for overseeing the day-to-day management of the project. They have the authority to make changes to the project's constraints.

- **Team:** The project team is responsible for ensuring that the project's products and services are of high quality. They have the necessary skills and knowledge to manage the project's various tasks and constraints.

- **Assurance:** Although the board is usually delegated to oversee the project's management, project assurance is a requirement that is independent from the project manager. This type of assurance ensures that the project is being managed properly.

- **Support:** The role may involve providing administrative assistance to the board and the project manager. It can also include the supervision and guidance of the project's control and planning systems. Depending on the skills and experience of the board member, the role may involve providing advice and guidance.

Project Management Using SharePoint Communication Sites

One of the most important factors that businesses consider when it comes to technology is the availability of software such as Microsoft's SharePoint Online for content management. This is why more companies are turning to this solution to manage their projects. This section covers the various features of SharePoint communication sites and how they can help you achieve success.

As you learned, the process of organizing and planning a project using Microsoft's SharePoint server is known as project management. SharePoint can help businesses improve their efficiency and manage their projects from start to finish. With the help of this platform, businesses can share files and collaborate on projects in real time.

The popularity of Microsoft's platform for project management continues to rise. Through its customizable settings and intuitive interface, it can be tailored to meet the needs of different teams and organizations. This allows teams to create a specific location for all of their tasks and documents.

With built-in reporting features, users can easily track their project's progress and identify areas for improvement. This platform can help improve team communication and lead to successful outcomes.

With the help of Microsoft's platform, teams can collaborate and share documents in a secure environment. It also has various features that allow users to track their projects.

With the help of custom workflows and lists, users can create a variety of tools that allow them to manage their projects and keep track of their tasks. They can also use social media tools to keep their team members updated on the progress of their projects.

Project Management Best Practices Using SharePoint Communication Sites

There are multiple modules in a project that can be handled using communication sites. From setting alerts, to publishing dashboards, to managing content, to tracking resources, communication sites can be adopted in many ways for effective project management. Here are some best practices:

- **Manage alerts:** One of the most common issues that teams face when it comes to project management is the lack of communication between team members. With the advanced alert functions in Microsoft, they can easily track the progress of their projects and notify their team members when changes or tasks are made. However, this can lead to a workflow breakdown.

- **Reports:** One of the most important factors that teams should consider when it comes to implementing project reporting is Microsoft's platform, which can be easily customized and embedded into pages. With the help of various filters and dashboards, users can easily find the data they need. Additionally, automatic email notifications can be sent to team members to keep them informed about the status of their projects.

- **Content management:** With the help of SharePoint
  communication sites, users can easily collect and
  aggregate data from various project sites. This can
  help them identify potential issues and improve the
  efficiency of their projects. One of the most common
  issues that teams face when it comes to project
  management is the lack of data synchronization.
  This can happen when multiple teams or individuals
  work on different projects and store data in different
  locations. Having a central location where all of the
  necessary data is stored can help make it easier for
  team members to access and complete their projects.

- **Dashboard:** Despite the increasing number of data
  collected and analyzed by businesses, most employees
  still lack the necessary skills to use it. One of the most
  effective ways to improve the efficiency of a company
  is by having a dashboard summary. This type of
  document provides a high-level overview of the various
  data points that a company collects. It can be used as
  an executive summary or a weekly report for managers.
  A dashboard is an easy-to-read and comprehensive
  overview of key performance indicators and other
  data that can be used to make informed decisions.
  It can be combined with graphics to provide a visual
  presentation of the information.

- **Project communication:** SharePoint communication
  sites can be used by businesses to keep track of
  their employees and improve the communication
  between them. They can be customized to meet the

needs of a company. It is important to learn how
to use the various features in order to improve the
communication between workers and clients. One of
the most effective ways to improve the efficiency of a
company is by having a communication tool that can
help manage the various tasks and projects that a team
member is involved in. With the help of this type of
tool, everyone can easily follow the same process and
keep their tasks and projects on track.

- **Managing resources:** One of the most critical tasks
  that businesses face when it comes to managing their
  resources is ensuring that they have an effective system
  in place. There are several ways that you can use
  SharePoint communications sites to get the most out of
  your resources.

- **Goal setting:** One of the most effective ways to set goals
  is through the use of SharePoint communication sites.
  This can be done by creating a goal list, which is an
  easy way to see all of your goals in one place. You can
  also add details such as the date that you want to reach
  the goal, or a link to the information that you want
  to share

- **Visual tracking:** SharePoint communication sites can
  display timelines, which are a visual representation of
  the history of events or changes that have occurred in
  a page. This can be useful when you need to track the
  progress of a project or when you want to show a page's
  history of changes.

- **Schedule kick-off meetings and avoid unproductive meetings:** Kickoff meetings are a great way to get started on a project, and Office helps you manage your schedule and keep track of who has shown up and who has declined. You can also send out meeting agendas and keep track of meeting minutes with the help of a calendar feature in Office. Unfortunately, meetings can be very disruptive to the workplace. Unproductive meetings can be very frustrating for everyone involved. There are a few things that can be done to prevent them from happening, and these can help make them more productive. First, set an agenda and make sure that everyone is in attendance. Second, avoid having conversations that are not related to the topic. Finally, make sure that everyone is following the discussion.

One of the most important factors that businesses consider when it comes to project management is the availability of Microsoft's SharePoint platform. It provides a wide range of features and functions, such as a Document Library, a calendar, and discussion boards. It can also be used to create websites, manage employee profiles, and create projects. Because it is a Microsoft product, it can be integrated with other applications, such as Outlook and Excel.

SharePoint Online Communication Sites Use Case for Project Management

This section explores the features of SharePoint communication sites and demonstrates its adoption to project management using a use case. The following are some steps in a project setup process that can be handled using SharePoint Communication sites:

1. Create a new site for a project.

2.   Create a list to management project-related items.

3.   Track different ongoing projects.

4.   Create automated workflows to trigger notifications.

5.   Allocate work using a SharePoint list.

6.   Manage resources.

7.   Update status reports and use the Project Dashboard.

The following sections cover each of these steps in more detail.

Creating a New Site for a Project

It's smart to create a nice-looking communication site for your users that allows them to manage their projects. For instance, at the home page of ABC site (see Figure 6-1), you can easily access all the details about the projects that you're working on. There's also a link icon that takes you to the Project Dashboard.

Figure 6-1. Project home page

On this page, you can access all of the tools and data that you need to work on your project. We used a webpart in order to create a communication site that includes a New Project Set Up Form and a data list. There are also a variety of dashboards built on top of the data stored in the database.

Creating a List to Management Project-Related Items

The new project data list in Microsoft's SharePoint platform allows business development and sales teams to keep track of all the new projects that they are working on. It also allows them to manage their key metrics, such as the number of new projects and the status of their client information. Figure 6-2 shows an example SharePoint list containing information such as content title, description, author, status, and due date.

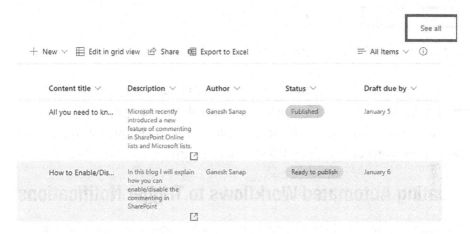

Figure 6-2. *List creation*

Tracking Different Ongoing Projects

In SharePoint communication sites, you can track and search all the necessary information about a project that you need to complete, as shown in Figure 6-3a. You can set up the data that you need in this list in the navigation menu, as shown in Figure 6-3b. From the top navigation bar, you can easily access the project's information.

Project Tasks

Today		October 29		November 4		November 10		November 16	November 22	November 28

Initiate the Project	Plan and Setup the Project	Work the Project		Track and Re-Plan the Project	Close the Project
10/24 - 10/31	11/1 - 11/8	11/9 - 11/16		11/19 - 11/26	11/27 - 12/4

Stop editing this list

All Tasks   Active Tasks   Calendar   ···

✓	☑	Task Name		Start Date	Finish Date	Task Status	Assigned To	+
	☐	⊿ Initiate the Project ⧉	···	Today	October 31	In Progress	☐ Billy Guinan	
	☑	~~Get the Project Approved,~~ ~~Sponsored, and Resourced~~ ⧉	···	Today	October 31	Completed	☐ Billy Guinan	
	☐	~~Decide a Project Management~~	···					

Figure 6-3a. *Tracking projects*

Figure 6-3b. *Searching projects*

You can easily find all the information you need about a project by searching all the projects in the list. You can also create a new project and edit all the details at once. This feature has been very popular among users. With flows, you can create codeless functionalities such as notifications.

Creating Automated Workflows to Trigger Notifications

With the help of a tool like SharePoint, you can automate the workflow between multiple roles within a company or department. SharePoint can also send notifications to people when you trigger a certain event in the system.

Say for example that Sales wants to notify Operations about the new project that it has sold. This process involves sending multiple emails to the people who are involved in the project. The goal of these emails is to let them know about the new project's details so they can pass the baton to the next generation.

If you open my email inbox, you will see that I have a new project notification request, as shown in Figure 6-4. This is an approval email that's coming from the sales team manager, who owns the workflow, and he wants to make sure that the operations team knows about the new project.

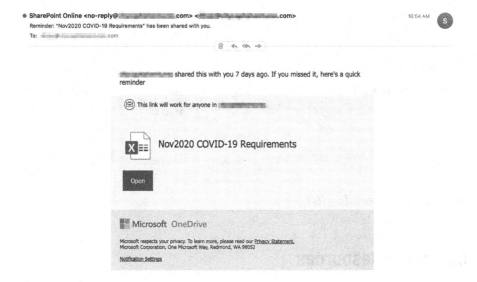

Figure 6-4. *Email notification*

Allocating Work Using SharePoint List

The Work Log feature automatically sets up a new list in Microsoft. When it is created, it is automatically associated with a project and can be deleted or archived. This is useful for keeping all the details about the project in one place. See Figure 6-5. You can also notify the team and link back to the project from the home page.

✓	☑	Task Name		Start Date	Finish Date	Task Status
	☑	◢ Initiate the Project	⋯	**December 2, 2019**	**December 6, 2019**	**Completed**
	☑	Get the Project Approved, Sponsored, and Resourced	⋯	December 2, 2019	December 6, 2019	Completed
	☑	Decide a Project Management Process	⋯	December 2, 2019	December 6, 2019	Completed
	☑	Create a Collaborative Project Site	⋯	December 2, 2019	December 6, 2019	Completed
	☑	◢ Plan and Setup the Project	⋯	**December 9, 2019**	**December 18, 2019**	**Completed**
	☑	Plan the Project	⋯	December 9, 2019	December 13, 2019	Completed
	☑	Desk Check the Project Plan	⋯	December 16, 2019	December 16, 2019	Completed
	☑	Assign tasks to the team	⋯	December 17, 2019	December 18, 2019	Completed
	☐	◢ Work the Project	⋯	**Today**	**March 31**	Not Started
	☑	◢ Weekly team meetings ¤	⋯	**Today**	**March 31**	Completed ▾
	☑	Book room for weekly meeting ¤	⋯	4 days ago	3 days ago	Completed
	☑	Share agenda for meeting with the team ¤	⋯	4 days ago	3 days ago	Completed

Figure 6-5. *Work log list*

Managing Resources

The Operations Manager can assign key resources to a project from the screen. Figure 6-6 shows how to assign a project manager, a senior manager, and their managers. As you assign people, they will receive an email notification.

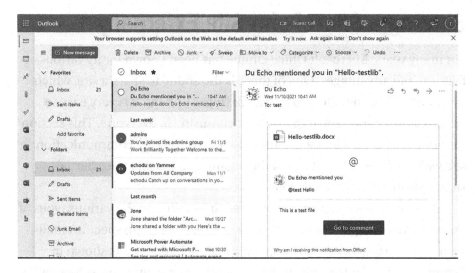

Figure 6-6. *Project assignment*

Using the Status Update and Project Dashboard

The Project Manager can now view all the details about the project, including the date it was logged, its budget, and its actual hours. They can also enter their own details, such as their forecast and budget. If they click the link, they will get the information from the source in Microsoft's SharePoint.

The workflow will notify the team members if there are any changes to the project information. This ensures that everyone has the latest information. It also helps minimize the time that team members have to gather for meetings.

You will receive various benefits using this system, such as being able to work with more effective and efficient employees, having better relationships with your sales and operations, and reducing errors.

Sharing a SharePoint Site Externally

For many years, Microsoft Office Online has been known for its various features and advantages. One of these is the ability to share a site, which is very different from file and folder sharing. Although it is very easy to share a site in a browser, it can be very confusing to everyone. This section discusses about how to successfully share a SharePoint communication site with other people outside of the organization, using the external sharing feature in Microsoft 365.

Sharing files and folders via external links relies on the various types of links that you can generate. For instance, users can share specific emails with specific recipients using a specific People Link type, as shown in Figure 6-7. In order to confirm their identity, the recipient must enter a unique eight-digit passcode.

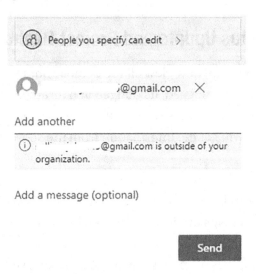

Figure 6-7. *External sharing*

If enabled, anonymity allows recipients to access shared folders and files without requiring them to type in passcodes. This method works even if the recipient has the link type enabled.

Regardless of which option you choose, the process is relatively simple and painless for both the recipient and the originator. Unlike sharing files and folders in a web browser, doing so in a secure environment such as Microsoft 365 requires the recipient to provide a unique identity.

Instead of sending eight-digit codes, users must enter a Microsoft ID and an email address to confirm their identity. After they accept the invite, the users will see their name and address in the User directory of Microsoft 365 or Azure.

Enabling External Sharing in SharePoint

Here are steps for enabling access in SharePoint for external users:

Step 1: Access the Microsoft 365 Admin Center, as shown in Figure 6-8.

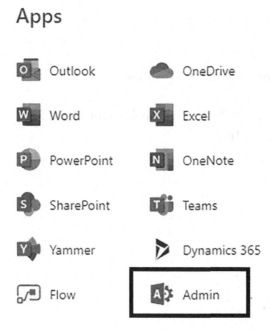

Figure 6-8. *M365 Admin access*

Step 2: Access SharePoint from the Admin Center, as shown in Figure 6-9.

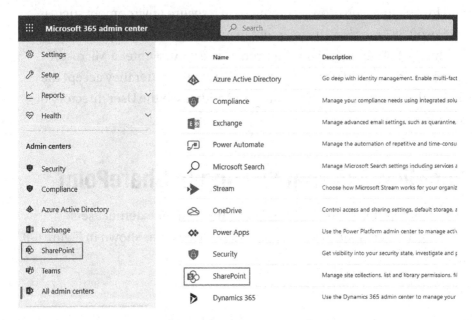

Figure 6-9. *SharePoint admin center*

Step 3: Choose the Sharing option from the SharePoint Admin Center, as shown in Figure 6-10.

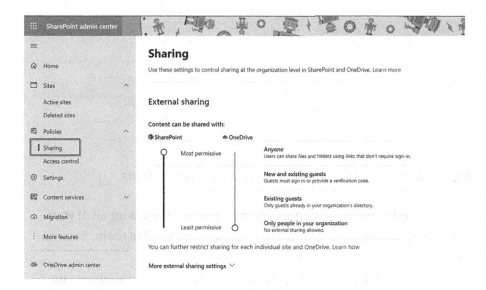

Figure 6-10. *SharePoint Sharing feature*

Step 4: Determine how content will be shared, as shown in Figure 6-11. Be sure you understand the various external sharing options, as listed in Figure 6-12.

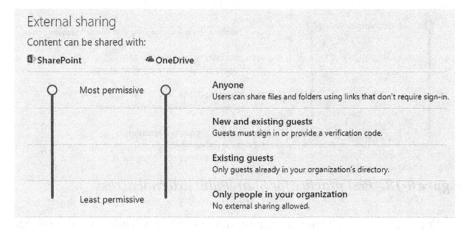

Figure 6-11. *External sharing overview*

Figure 6-12. *Understand the external sharing options*

This section allows you to set up tenant-wide settings for all of your sites. These settings will automatically be applied to all of them. You can also set site-level sharing settings.

You will notice that making Microsoft Office Online available to new and existing guests will restrict the sharing of files in the cloud. The best practice is as shown in Figure 6-13.

Figure 6-13. *Best practice for SharePoint external access*

You can also set site-level sharing settings. This will allow you to enable external sharing for certain groups of users but prevent it at the site level.

Sites that follow the default tenant setting will be more permissive than those that do not.

SharePoint Experience for External Users

An external recipient of the email in Figure 6-14 will likely receive it in the junk or spam folder. Advise your guests to check it in there as well. The email will be received from no-reply@sharpointonline.com and will look like Figure 6-14.

Figure 6-14. *Email invitation to guest*

When these external users click Next, they will see Figure 6-15.

Welcome to SharePoint Online

Microsoft account
Sign in with the account you use for OneDrive, Xbox LIVE, Outlook.com, or other Microsoft services.

Organizational account
Sign in with the account provided by your work or school to use with Office 365 or other Microsoft services.

Don't have either account? Create a Microsoft account, it's quick and easy!

Figure 6-15. *External user screen*

External users have three options:

- This scenario is usually used by an organization that has an Microsoft 365 subscription. The recipient can then log in to their company's website using their user ID. After clicking the link, the external user will be prompted to enter their Microsoft 365 credentials.

- The recipient can still use their existing Microsoft account even if they don't have an Microsoft 365 subscription. For instance, the user might have an account for Xbox.com or Outlook.com. They can also create a new account for various other services, such as Hotmail.com.

- If the recipient does not have an existing Microsoft account, a new one can be created on the fly. Just enter the required details and click Create New Account. It's very quick and easy to set up.

Once the external user's request is accepted, that user can access the SharePoint communication sites.

Summary

In this chapter, you learned about project management using SharePoint communication sites, some uses case for project management activities, and external sharing using SharePoint communication sites. The next chapter explains seamless integration of SharePoint communication sites with Microsoft 365 products such as Forms, Power Apps, Power Automate, and Teams.

CHAPTER 7

Integrating SharePoint Communication Sites with Microsoft 365 Products

Microsoft 365 services offers a seamless experience among its many products. Although they are different in look and feel and have different designs, the user experience remains the same. This chapter explores the seamless integration experience of SharePoint communication sites with Microsoft Forms, Power Apps, Power Automate, and Teams, to kick off your journey through this seamless experience.

Seamless Integration Between SharePoint Communication Sites and Microsoft Forms

This section explores the seamless integration with SharePoint communication sites and Microsoft built in the Microsoft 365 space. In this section, we demonstrate Microsoft Forms creation within and outside a communication site. For a case that's outside a communication site, we also explain how do bring such forms back into SharePoint communication sites.

Creating a New Form in Communication Site

Microsoft Forms can be created in communication sites using the Forms webpart. Using this webpart, you can create multiple forms in a communication site and make them accessible through this communication site. Although the form is built in a communication site, you can share it with wider audience. Use the following steps to create a new form using the webpart available in the SharePoint communication sites.

Step 1: Create a new page. Go the site where you want to add the page and click the +New menu, as shown in Figure 7-1, to create a new page.

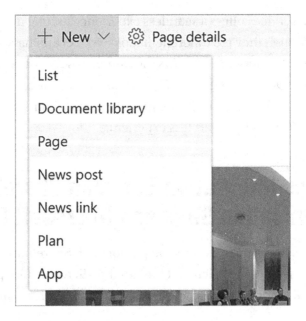

Figure 7-1. *Create new page*

Step 2: Choose the visuals of your choice, as shown in Figure 7-2.

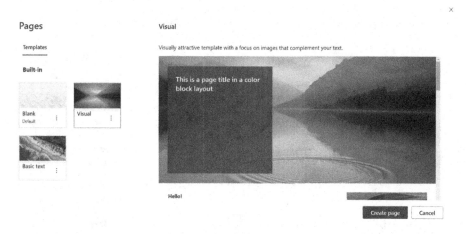

Figure 7-2. *Choose your visuals*

Step 3: Click the Create Page button shown in Figure 7-2 to create your new page. After this, hover your mouse over the title area. You will see a + with a circle, as shown in Figure 7-3, which is how you add the webpart.

Figure 7-3. *Add a webpart*

Step 4: Once you click +, a popup page will open containing all the webparts, as shown in Figure 7-4.

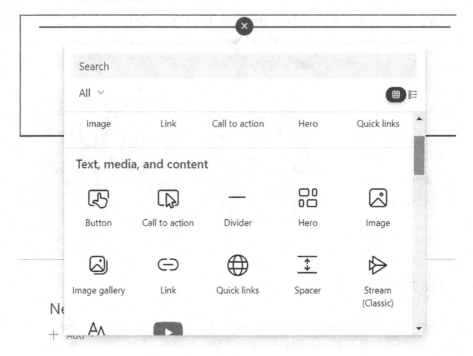

Figure 7-4. *The pop-up window containing all the webparts in
communication sites*

Step 5: Search for the Forms webpart and click it, as shown in
Figure 7-5.

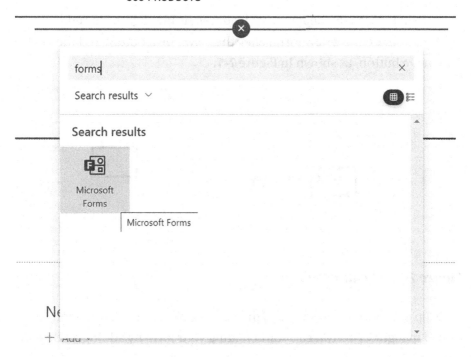

Figure 7-5. *Choose the Microsoft Forms webpart*

Step 6: Once you choose the Forms webpart, there will be two
options—one to create a new form and another to use an existing form—as
shown in Figure 7-6.

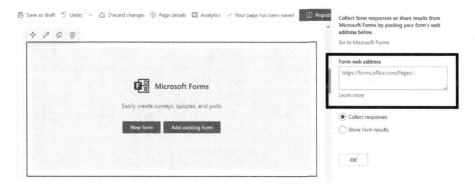

Figure 7-6. *Choose or create a form*

Also in Figure 7-6, the form's web address is highlighted in red.

Step 7: To create a new form, click the New Form button and then click the Create button, as shown in Figure 7-7.

Figure 7-7. *Creating a form*

Step 8: Once you click Create, the Forms Creation page will open, as shown in Figure 7-8. You can start creating your form by adding a title—in our case Test.

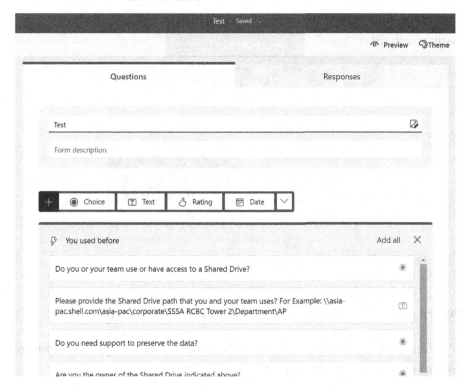

Figure 7-8. *Forms creation page*

Finally, once you save the page created in Step 1, the form will be
displayed in this page.

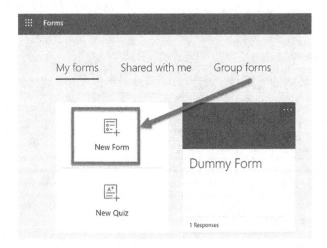

Figure 7-9. *Create a new form without use of a webpart*

Then, enter all details, such as the form name and the questions part of
the form, as shown in Figure 7-10.

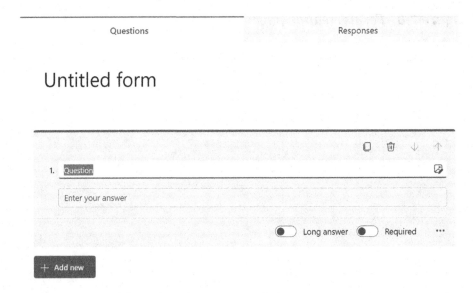

Figure 7-10. *Adding details to a new form*

In Step 8, if you click Select and choose an existing form button, a page appears where you can add a Form ID. This ID will be displayed in the page showing forms results and form responses, as shown in Figure 7-11.

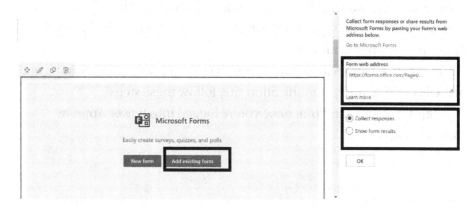

Figure 7-11. *Clicking the Add Existing Form button*

You should now be able to create forms in the communication sites and you've witnessed the seamless integration experience between SharePoint communication sites and Microsoft Forms.

Seamless Integration Between SharePoint Communication Sites and Power Apps

This section shows you how to create a Canvas app using Power Apps and Microsoft Lists. You can do this from within either Power Apps or Microsoft Online.

The app will have three screens—the Browse, Details, and Edit screens. The Browse screen allows you to view all the details about a single item in the list, while the Details screen shows all the information about that item. The Edit screen allows you to update or create an existing item.

Even if you create a list that's very complex, the principles of creating
an app will not change. The app will still have the same features regardless
of the complexity of the list. In this section, we create an app from Power
Apps and SharePoint Online (i.e., from a list part of the SharePoint
communication). This will demonstrate the seamless nature of Power
Apps and communication sites.

To create an app within Power Apps based on information coming out
of the list part of the communication site, follow these steps:

Step 1: Select SharePoint once you're logged into Power Apps, as
shown in Figure 7-12.

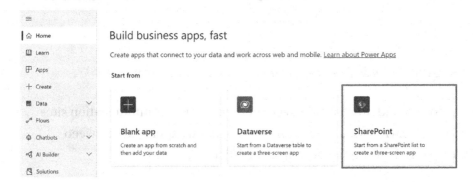

Figure 7-12. *Selecting the Sharepoint option from the Power
Apps Console*

Step 2: Once you click SharePoint, the page shown in Figure 7-13 will
page appear.

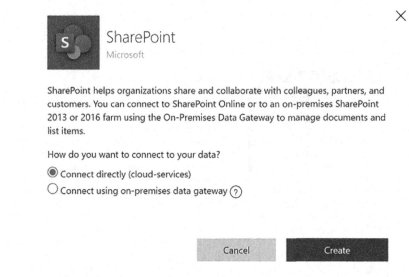

Figure 7-13. Creating the app

Step 3: Once you click the Create button in Figure 7-13, a window
will pop up, where you enter the name of the app. Select a SharePoint
communication site or a on-premises SharePoint site. From this
communication, select a SharePoint List, as shown in Figure 7-14. Finally,
click the Create button.

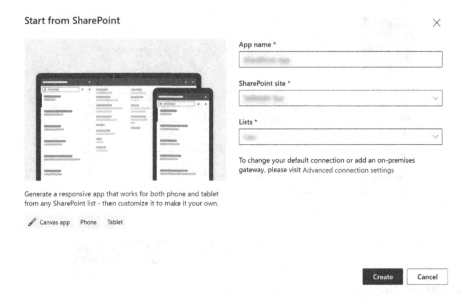

Figure 7-14. *Enter the app details*

Step 4: After you click the Create button, all processing will start, and
the app is created with information coming from the communication list.
See Figure 7-15.

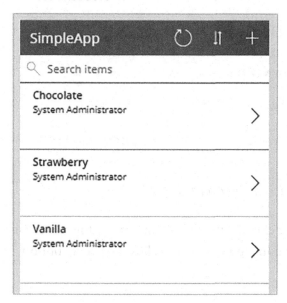

Figure 7-15. *App created based on the SharePoint list*

The app will automatically show the data in more columns if your
list has multiple entries. On the top of the screen, there are icons that will
allow you to sort the list, create an item, and refresh the list. A search box
will also allow you to filter the list based on text.

Next, you will create Power Apps using SharePoint Online.

The app will automatically appear as a view when you open it in
SharePoint Online. You can also run it in a web browser, on an Android
device, or on an iOS device.

Step 1: Access any document library, then choose Integrate➤Power
Apps ➤ Create an App, as shown in Figure 7-16.

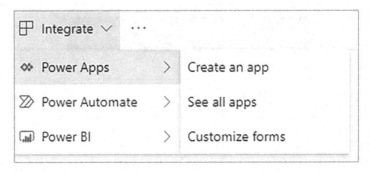

Figure 7-16. *Creating an app*

Step 2: After clicking the Create an App button, enter the app name in
the panel shown in Figure 7-17 and click the Create button.

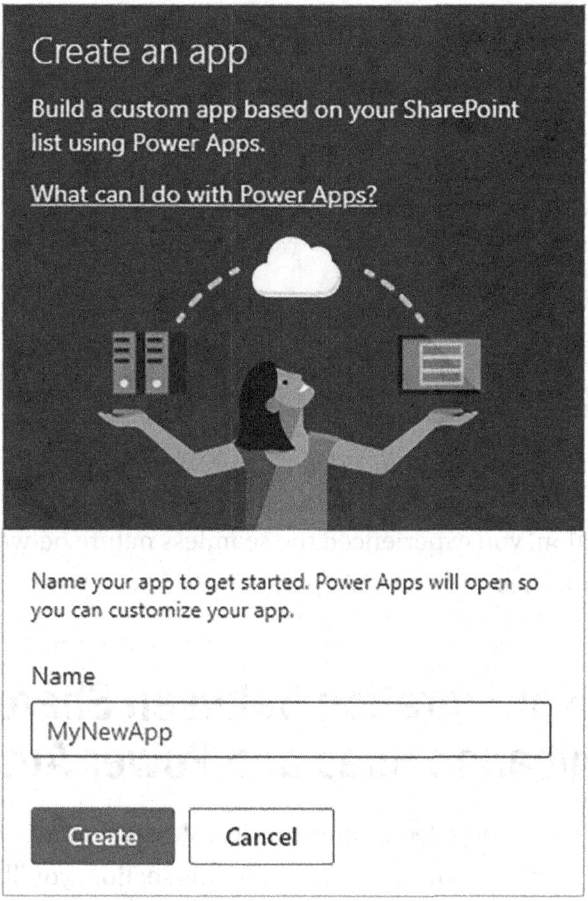

Figure 7-17. *Enter the app's name*

Step 3: The app is created, as shown in Figure 7-18.

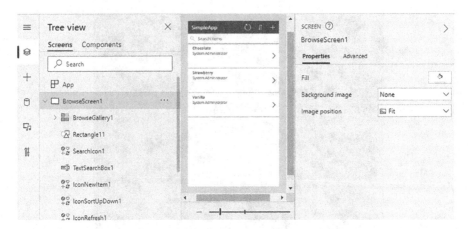

Figure 7-18. *App creation in Power Apps from SharePoint*

In this section, you experienced the seamless nature between communication sites and Power Apps.

Seamless Integration Between SharePoint Communication Sites and Power Automate

Chapter 8 includes a detailed example of seamless integration between SharePoint Online and Power Automate. In this section, you'll see how to enable data flows from Power Automate and data flows from SharePoint communication sites to demonstrate the seamless experience between them.

First, let's kickstart flow creation in SharePoint Communication sites by following these steps:

Step 1: Access any document library and then click Create a Flow, as shown in Figure 7-19.

Figure 7-19. *Choose the Create a Flow option*

Step 2: Choose the flow you need, as shown in Figure 7-20.

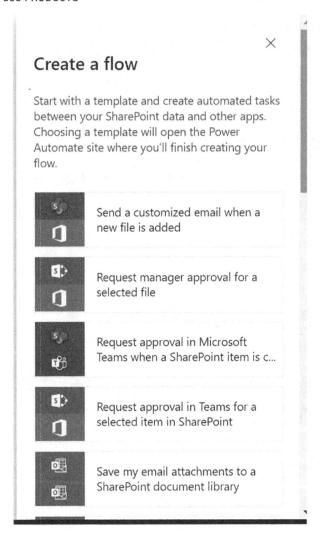

Figure 7-20.   List of flows

If you select the first option, which is called Send a Customized Email
When A New File Is Added, then you need to set up the configuration
settings such as SharePoint Link, document library selection, and email
customization in order for the flow to be executed successfully, as shown
in Figure 7-21.

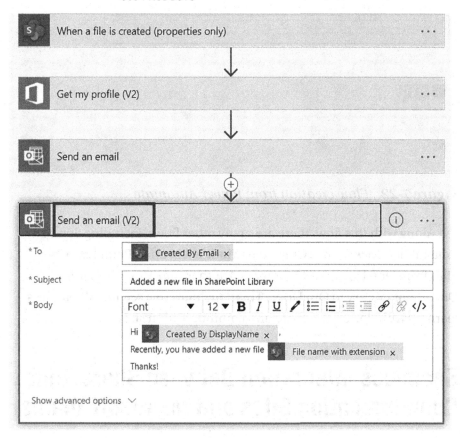

Figure 7-21. *Flow configuration*

Similarly, this flow can created from Power Automate. To do so, access
Powerautomate.microsoft.com and search for Send a Customized Email
When A New File Is Added, as shown in Figure 7-22. Finally, you end up
configuring communication site details and customizing communication,
as shown in Figure 7-22.

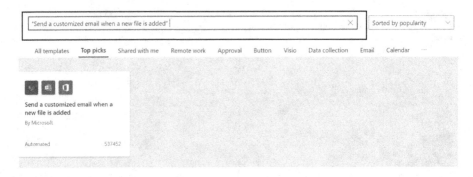

Figure 7-22. *Flow creation from Power Automate*

Along with this flow, there are many other flows, including Send an Email When New Item Is Created or Modified in SharePoint List, Copy Files from One Document Library to Another, and Move Files from Document Library to OneDrive. This concludes this section of seamless learning with Power Automate and communication sites.

Seamless Integration Between SharePoint Communication Sites and Microsoft Teams

OneDrive is very similar to the My Folder concept on standard laptops. You store attachments that you diligently share with colleagues when there is a need and you do not share them with all colleagues. For example, Salary Slips, Project Manuals, ID Card Soft Copies, and others.

So far, you have learned that SharePoint Online is used for content collaboration with wider audiences. Files that you host on SharePoint Online are not limited to a few people. In fact, a substantial number of people access files shared through SharePoint Online in Figure 7-23. Examples including marketing collaterals, news, and organization charts.

Figure 7-23. *File experience in Microsoft 365*

Therefore, OneDrive is used to share documents for very specific purposes and with people whom you choose. On the other hand, SharePoint Online is used to share documents with a wider audience.

An important point to remember is that whenever a file is uploaded in Microsoft 365, it is stored in SharePoint Online. Files shared through Teams Chat are hosted in OneDrive along with other files uploaded by the users.

In Figures 7-24 and 7-25, you see that whenever a file is uploaded through Teams, the conversation is stored in SharePoint and in the Teams Chat feature and then it is hosted in OneDrive.

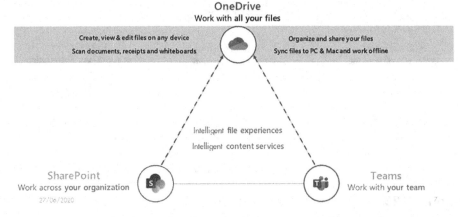

Figure 7-24. *Files hosted either in SharePoint Online and OneDrive are shared in the Teams conversation*

In Figure 7-24 shows that files already hosted either in SharePoint Online and OneDrive are shared in the Teams conversation. When you click the File Upload menu from Teams, there are three ways to access a file. You can access SharePoint Online, OneDrive, or a local drive. In Figure 7-25, things are subtly different, whereby files uploaded into Teams are stored in SharePoint Online and OneDrive into Teams.

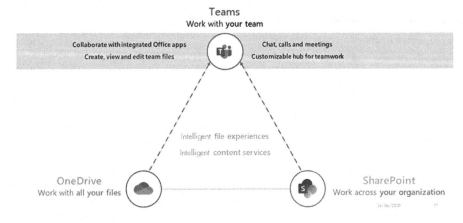

Figure 7-25. *Files uploaded to Teams are stored either in SharePoint Online or on OneDrive into Teams*

When a team is created, a corresponding SharePoint communication site is also created. The contents inside this SharePoint communication site can be managed via Teams and the SharePoint communication sites, thus offering a seamless experience.

Summary

Now that you've seen how seamless integration experiences between communication sites and Microsoft Forms, Power Apps, Power Automate, and Teams works, you end your journey of seamless experiences. In the next chapter, you will explore the usefulness of communication sites to perform project management activities.

CHAPTER 8

Creating New Horizons of Digital Communication

You have reached to last chapter of this book, and the focus continues to be on harnessing the benefits of communication sites. This chapter discusses the new horizon of digital communications, explores digital communication using Power Automate and communicate sites, explores user collaboration using Teams and communication sites, and looks at the new webparts you can use to design communication sites.

In 1969, the L0 message was sent between two computers at UCLA and Stanford. The event marked the beginning of a new era in computer-mediated communication. Although the message was supposed to be sent with the word LOGIN, the connection between the two computers was established even though it crashed.

ARPANET was not intended for communication. By the time people started using it for electronic messaging and instant messaging, it had become a standard part of their lives.

The early users of the Internet saw its potential as a communication tool. Due to the advancements in technology, sharing information between people who were geographically apart has become a common practice. Mobile communication and networked computers are prevalent in modern organizations.

© Charles David Waghmare 2023
C. D. Waghmare, *Beginning SharePoint Communication Sites*,
https://doi.org/10.1007/978-1-4842-8960-0_8

The rules and norms of digital interactions are different than those of traditional forms of communication. Despite the technological advancements that have occurred in digital business communication over the years, this concept is still evolving.

According to Holmes, a scholar who studies workplace interactions, communication in professional settings is a complex business. People have multiple goals when it comes to their interactions with coworkers. They need to maintain their social and professional relationships while also accomplishing their daily tasks.

The complexity of professional interactions is even more apparent in the virtual workplace, where people don't share the same physical environment. In order to maintain their professional relationships, all employees need to understand each other through their written messages.

Although it is not surprising that people have different strategies when it comes to communicating their goals and intentions, it is also important that their messages are understood and interpreted correctly. In the digital world, people can't use cues such as the tone of their voice or facial expressions to help them understand messages. Instead, they rely on written techniques and words to communicate their goals.

External communication has become more complex and interactive. The rise of social media, blogs, and collaborative sites has dramatically changed how organizations communicate with their external stakeholders. Before, messages from the top were typically delivered in a centralized manner. Now they are delivered through an interactive platform. According to corporate communication scholar Michael Cornelissen, the rapid emergence and evolution of new media has changed how organizations communicate. It is now more important than ever that they engage with their stakeholders in a way that is both informative and effective.

This is a concern for many organizations, as they now have to respond to their customers in an instant. They don't always have the time to thoroughly analyze and verify messages, yet these are the very messages that influence their reputation and business success.

Due to the rise of social media and the increasing scrutiny that businesses face, it is no surprise that they need to spend a lot of time and resources managing their communications. This can be done through the development of effective strategies and methods to collect and analyze data.

The rise of digital communication channels has created a need for businesses to have a clear understanding of their various communication channels and develop their employees' digital skills. According to Hulme, these individuals are now regarded as an asset to their organizations.

Due to the importance of corporate communication and the interactions that it creates, it is no surprise that communication skills have become a requirement in white-collar workplaces. In addition to being able to communicate effectively, good soft skills are also often regarded as an asset.

In addition, studies have shown that the lack of effective communication skills can lead to various issues such as failure in implementing projects. According to a survey, over 50 percent of strategic projects fail due to the lack of effective communication.

The survey also revealed that poor language use is one of the main factors that can prevent projects from achieving their goals. Despite the increasing importance of communication skills, traditional training programs are not always effective at developing these skills. Instead, they often focus on the development of a prescriptive approach. This approach doesn't provide the necessary help in developing a deeper understanding of language.

This is especially true in the case of digital media, as training materials that are geared toward keeping up with the rapid technological changes are often not acknowledged by academic research.

In today's professional environment, people have a wide variety of media to choose from, including video streaming and voice. Despite the availability of these channels, the number of people using text-based instant messaging (IM) is on the rise. According to a survey conducted by the Radicati group, the number of people using this type of messaging is expected to grow by over three billion by 2019.

According to a survey, over 80 percent of businesses have mandated the use of corporate-sanctioned instant messaging. This shows that the technology has become widely used in the workplace. It also allows employees to communicate with each other and with external clients.

Despite the increasing number of people using instant messaging, the negative effects of this technology are still widely debated. According to some studies, instant messaging can help reduce productivity and digital addiction. In fact, research has shown that it can also help improve interaction between two people.

Instant messaging allows employees to quickly communicate with each other and clarify their questions without disrupting the workflow. In virtual work environments, this type of technology can help create a shared space. The "line" is left open so that participants can communicate with each other on an as-needed basis.

For businesses, live chats are an appealing option due to their low cost and the ability to provide both synchronized and anonymous communication. This type of communication also allows customers to feel secure.

Due to the increasing popularity of instant messaging, there has been a lot of pressure placed on users to effectively use it. While it is a relatively complex communication channel, it is not as similar to other traditional forms of media. For instance, while email is commonly used to send and receive messages, IM is a hybrid between writing and speech.

This is because it is both informal and spontaneous, and it is also like writing because its transcript is searchable and has a permanent record. Besides being able to communicate in real time, IM also has the advantage of being able to provide various audiovisual cues. Here is an example of IM:

(1) [09:39] Chris: Hello Danny

(2) [09:39] Chris: How r u man?

(3) [09:39] Danny: Good evening, bro Chris

(4) [09:39] Danny: I am cool

(5) [09:39] Danny: Was your weekend cool?

(6) [09:40] Chris: Are you aware of any failures or missing things during last week?

(7) [09:40] Chris: No I cannot recollect.

(8) [09:41] Danny: Sorry I do not remember so; can you check with someone?

What's the strategy to use if your IM conversations are disrupted?

The previous script requires some skill to read, as the lines seem to be muddled up. In one-way IM systems, the partners construct their messages without knowing if the other person is still writing. As a result, the responses are often separated from the original message.

The messages that were delivered in the wrong order were caused by a lack of coordination. For instance, while Danny is talking about the weekend, Chris is already talking about a task-specific topic.

After sending the message, Chris may have noticed Danny's question in Line 5, and he may have provided an answer in Line 7. This is because, after talking about Danny's weekend, he asked more questions.

Although the team members of the virtual team have adopted the same practices as those in the real world, they are not able to translate these into instant messaging. For instance, how long should people talk to each other before the main topic is introduced? Also, what are the rules when it comes to disrupting a conversation?

The concept of instant communication has been questioned due to the various features that make it possible for people to communicate in real time. For instance, the persistent nature of the conversations and the ability to scroll have led to the emergence of new ways to communicate. In addition, the effects of a synchronicity and synchronization on how people use language have also been discussed.

For some time, IM was regarded as a type of synchronous communication tool because it required both participants to be logged on at the same time. However, people have recently started using it for other types of communication. For instance, some people use it for asynchronous or quasi-synchronous interactions.

One of the most common asynchronous techniques that people use IM for is the sticky note technique, which is mainly used in internal interactions. This type of communication allows the sender to type a message without expecting an immediate response.

Contextualizing Emotions and Intent

One of the most important factors that users need to consider when it comes to having a successful conversation is avoiding overlaps and gaps. In addition to being able to avoid these, users also need to include emotional and relational information in their conversations. This can be achieved through visual and auditory signals. A wide range of emotions and expressions can be easily detected in conversations, such as surprise, friendliness, sarcasm, and anger.

In order to convey the desired intent, users have to use the keyboard. They have done so in various creative ways throughout the evolution of computer-mediated communication.

The first study on the topic of "paralanguage" was published in 1980. It was conducted by John Carey. It covered various techniques that can help users communicate their feelings and modify the meanings of words. Since then, the field of communication has been continuously studied to learn how to use language to convey non-verbal meaning.

In Figure 8-1, you can see various forms of communication, such as acronyms and letter or number homophones. These are commonly used in a way that is not accurate or appropriate for the context. They are often referred to as "over-the-top" or "unconventional." They are also frequently misunderstood and are a source of interest among the media and researchers.

Figure 8-1. *Digital generation gap between ages*

Emoticons

There is no book on digital communication that doesn't have a section on emoticons. These are the symbols of computer-mediated conversations, and they have been around since the beginning of the digital age. Scott Fahlman, a computer scientist, reportedly invented them in 1982 as a way to signify jokes in discussion boards.

The use of emoticons has been regarded as a way to signal humorous intent since they were originally created to convey a message. They are commonly used in various forms of digital writing, such as email, instant messaging, and social media. This section aims to provide a comprehensive view of the work these symbols do, and it is also relevant to other forms of social media. One of the most important factors when it comes to observing the work these symbols do is to observe how users respond to them.

Emoticons are a controversial topic in business communication. Most communication books and guidelines discourage the use of them, with some arguing that they are overly familiar and unprofessional. However, in certain situations where a personal touch is required, including in online consultations or customer service chats, the use of emoticons can enhance interaction and lead to better customer satisfaction.

The ability to communicate effectively with one's emotions and friendly intent is an important part of motivating and influencing team members. Emotions can also be used in business-critical situations such as negotiations.

It's also important to consider the various scenarios that can arise when it comes to using emoticons. Unfortunately, most guidelines do not reflect the actual use of emoticons and are typically colored by the author's personal values. This is very important in training courses, where the guidelines are designed to be more normative.

Although emoticons can be used to convey a message's emotional content, they are not the only way to express feelings. In addition to being used to create a visual representation of people's emotions, other strategies can also be utilized to enhance the tone of written messages. For instance, letter repetition, ellipsis marks, and punctuation marks can all be utilized to enhance the presentation of various subtle interpersonal messages. Table 8-1 provides a summary of techniques that are commonly used in digital writing to enhance the tone of conversations.

Table 8-1. *Techniques to Express Emotion and Boost Interactivity*

Written Techniques

Non-lexical tokens	Hm, mm, oh, uh, ah, um, errr, erm, yup, yeah
Interjections and laughter	Boo, yuk, phew, oops, woah, awww, aaaa, eugh, hahaha, hehehe, hihi, hee hee
Comic strip sounds	Boing, boom, zzzz, grrrr, argh
Capitalization	All capital letters, lack of/presence of capitalization, unconventional capitalization
Spelling	Vocal spelling to imitate dialectal or casual pronunciation (yeez) Nonstandard spelling: letter repetitions—(loooong, gooood, morningggg)

Punctuation Techniques

Conventional use	As opposed to nonconventional (missing)
Repeated punctuation	Repetition and combination (!!!, !!?!) punctuation used as complete messages
Ellipsis mark	…
Other keyboard symbols	Brackets, underscores, *, and combinations

Unfortunately, many business communication training materials do not include proper emphasis techniques. They often have just one or two well-defined meanings of such techniques, and state that they are considered unprofessional.

Digital Communication Using SharePoint Communication Sites and Power Automate

The goal of this section is to show you how to create a page approval process in Microsoft 365 that will automate the approval process for all of your company's communications. This flow will allow you to create a list of news items that will be posted on your intranet and then extend them to other communication channels, such as email, Teams, and Yammer.

First, create a new item in the list part of your SharePoint communication sites and then follow this process to automate the communication between SharePoint communication sites and other M365 services of the company. This will allow you to create a list of items that can be extended to other communication channels, such as email, Teams, and Yammer. Currently, page approval flows can be accessed through the various communication sites in the system.

Here are the steps to create to a flow:

Step 1: Access flows from `Powerautomate.microsoft.com` and click New Flow from My flow section, as shown in Figure 8-2.

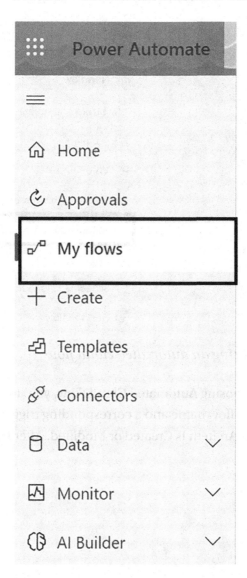

Figure 8-2. *Access the My Flows section to create a flow*

Step 2: Choose an existing template of flow by selecting Automated Cloud Flow, as shown in Figure 8-3.

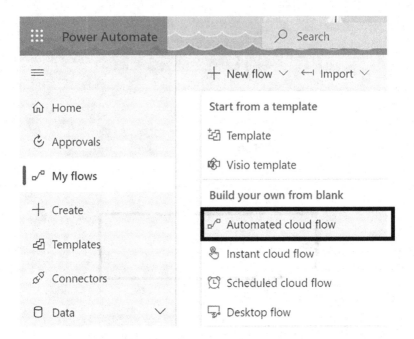

Figure 8-3.   *Choosing an automated cloud flow*

Step 3: After choosing Automated Cloud Flow, you'll see the screen in Figure 8-4. Add a flow name and a corresponding trigger. In this case, we are using When An Item Is Created or Modified. After this, click the Create button.

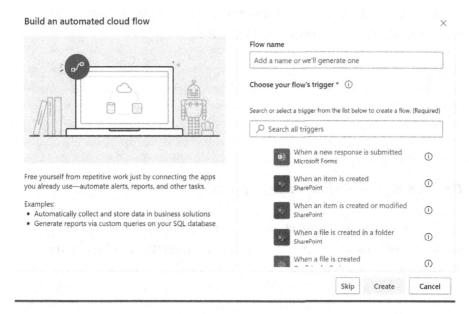

Figure 8-4. *Add a flow name and its trigger*

Step 4: After you create the flow, the screen in Figure 8-5 will appear. This will force you to add the SharePoint communicate sites link and its corresponding list. The flow will be triggered based on the addition of the item in the list and will push an email notification.

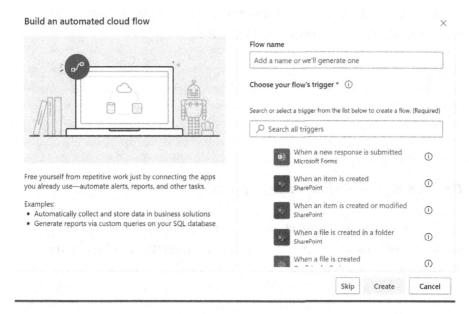

Figure 8-5. *Add the SharePoint communication site details*

Step 5: In order to retrieve the flow owner's profile, add a new step called Get My Profile, as shown in Figure 8-6.

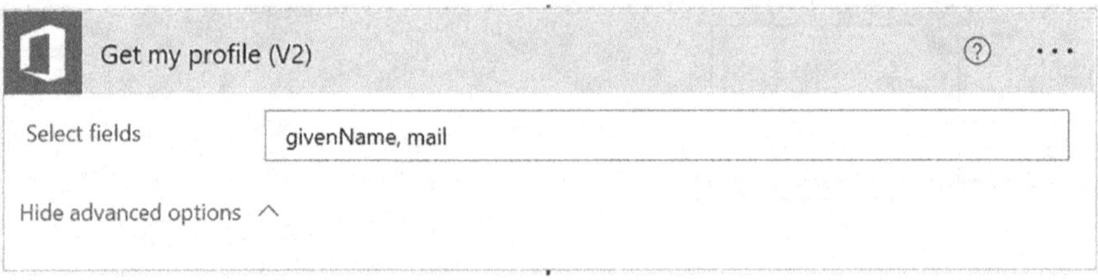

Figure 8-6. *Get the flow owner's profile*

Step 6: Add a Condition step, which indicates who you want to send this automated communication to, based on the new item in the SharePoint list. See Figure 8-7.

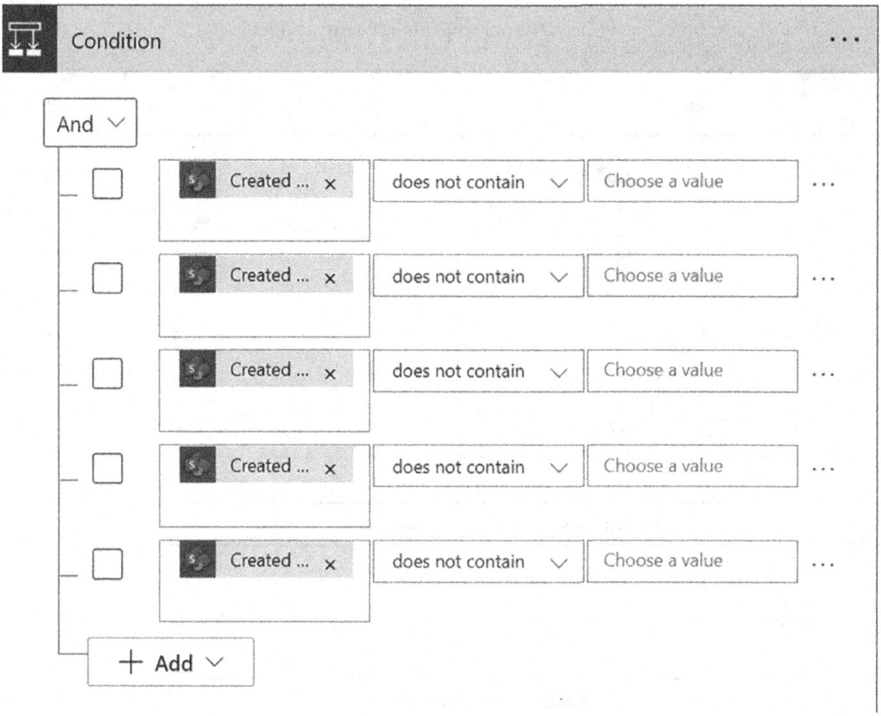

Figure 8-7. *Add users to receive notification*

Step 7: Configure a custom email communication by adding the email
step shown in Figure 8-8.

Figure 8-8. *Update the custom communication*

Using these steps, you can create a flow to publish emails to specific users when a new item is created in the SharePoint communication sites list. Further, instead of using email in Step 7, you can chose Yammer or MS Teams as well, in order to publish digital communication. This way, Power Automate with flow and SharePoint communication sites can be used to create digital, automated communications.

Using Teams and SharePoint Communications for User Collaboration

There are many ways to combine the power of Microsoft Teams and the magic of the web content management system, and it's hard to choose just one. But let's say that you have a team in Microsoft Teams. What can you do to make it even better?

A standard list in SharePoint displays a list of vendors and the individuals who are responsible for them (see Figure 8-9). Can you add a tab in Microsoft Teams as well? Before you can add a new tab, you need to make sure that the list in SharePoint communication sites has been created correctly.

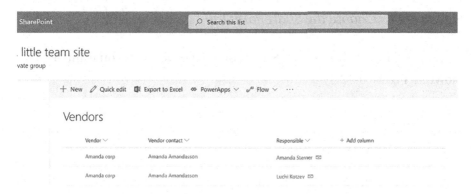

Figure 8-9. *SharePoint communication sites list of vendors*

To create a SharePoint tab in Teams, follow these steps:

Step 1: Click the + button in Teams and choose SharePoint, as shown in Figures 8-10 and 8-11.

Figure 8-10. *Add a tab with the + icon*

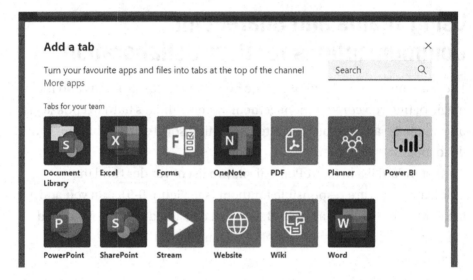

Figure 8-11. *Choose the SharePoint tab*

Step 2: Choose the specific SharePoint list of vendors you want, as shown in Figure 8-12.

Figure 8-12. *Choose the SharePoint list*

Step 3: Once you save the list, it will appear in Teams, as shown in Figure 8-13.

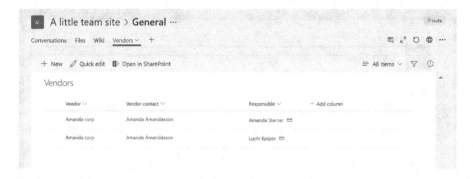

Figure 8-13. *List of vendors in Teams*

This way, users can collaborate on the same list of vendors in SharePoint and Teams and experience digital collaboration. Any update to the list is made in SharePoint and Teams.

Effectively Using SharePoint Communication Sites Webparts

This section explores some newly launched webparts that can add functionality to your communication sites.

The Text Webpart

The Text webpart allows you to add various types of text and images to your site, such as pull quotes and bullets, as shown in Figure 8-14. It has a variety of customization options:

- Alignment
- Bullets
- Idents
- Color, highlight, and text styles
- Table styles, alignment, and manipulation

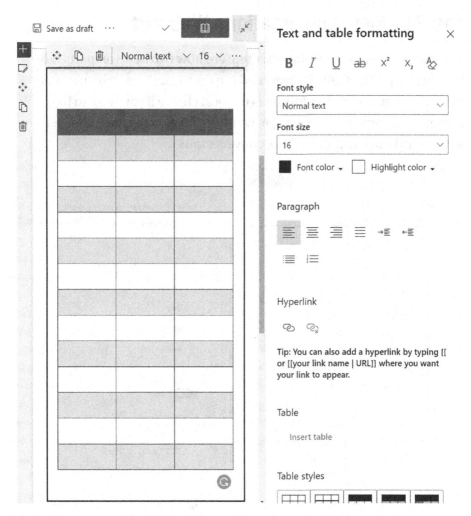

Figure 8-14. *The Text webpart*

This component is ideal for adding text-based content to a page without using various other webparts.

The Yammer Conversations Webpart

In addition to the usual webparts, there are now two new webparts for Yammer—the Highlights (newer) and the Conversations webparts—as shown in Figure 8-15. The former is the best choice if you want to have conversation right inside the page, while the latter is the ideal choice if you want users to participate in these conversations.

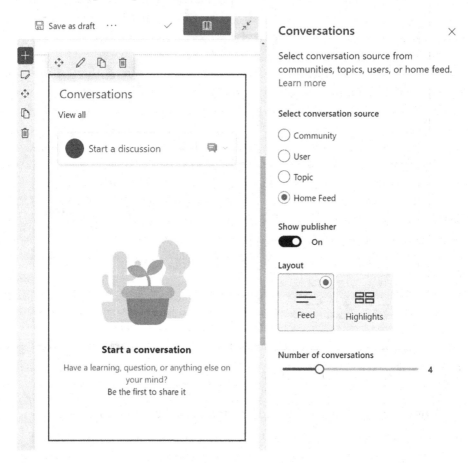

Figure 8-15. *The Yammer Conversation webpart*

The Conversations webpart allows to choose from various categories of conversations, such as Community, Home Feed, and User. It also allows you to display the publish and highlight features, as well as adjust the number of conversations that appear.

The Spacer Webpart

Adding whitespace to your page is very easy to do, and it makes it easier to read text and prevents your eyes from getting too tired. See Figure 8-16. You can also use the Spacer webpart to add empty space between various webparts.

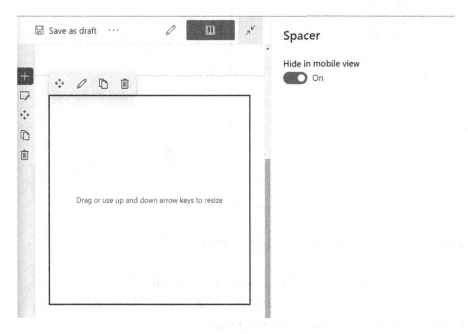

Figure 8-16. *The Spacer webpart*

The Saved for Later Webpart

Using this webpart, you can easily save documents, news articles, and pages on your mobile app. With the Saved for Later webpart, you can show users the documents and pages that have been saved for later, as shown in Figure 8-17.

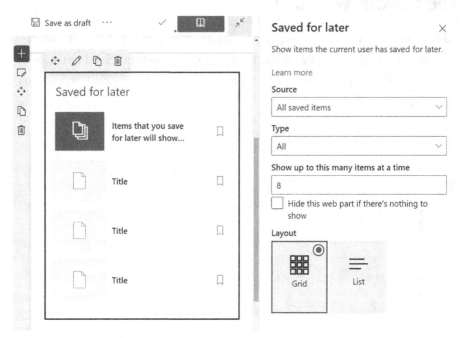

Figure 8-17. *The Saved for Later webpart*

You can also customize the webpart by adding the following information: the source of the saved files, the type of files saved, and the number of items that can be shown at once.

Unfortunately, this feature is not available to guest users of your website. They can use the items from the Saved for Later feature, but the item will not be shown here.

The Recent Documents Webpart

The Recent Documents webpart can be shown on the website's home page. It displays the most recent documents that users have accessed, as shown in Figure 8-18. This feature can also update as the user navigates through the various documents that are stored on the site.

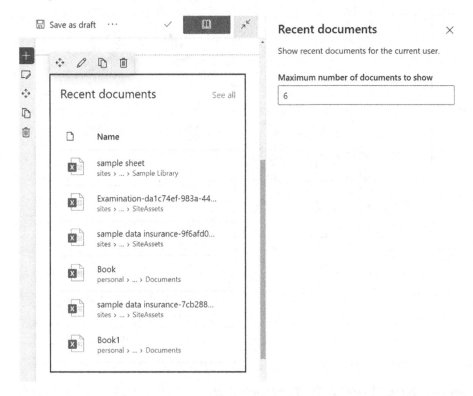

Figure 8-18. *The Recent Documents webpart*

The Quick Chart Webpart

If you need to show a simple pie or column chart on a page, the Quick Chart webpart is a good option, as shown in Figure 8-19. It can be used instead of creating a new chart in Excel or Power BI. You can also enter your own data or get it from an existing library or list.

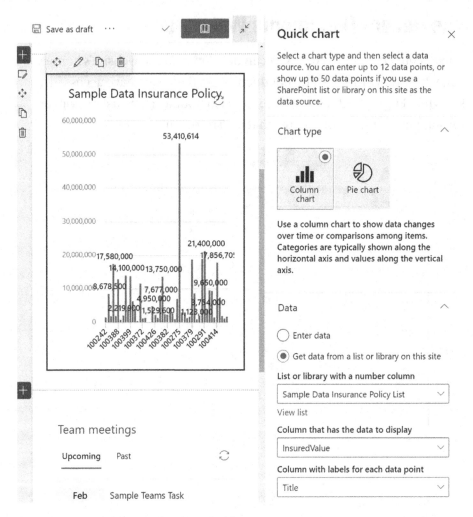

Figure 8-19. *The Quick Chart webpart*

The chart can also contain various elements that will be used to display the data in a column. These include the type of label used to indicate the data points in the column. The other elements can be used to sort the data and create labels.

The Microsoft PowerApps Webpart

Using Microsoft PowerApps, you can create web apps that are designed to work seamlessly with a browser, as shown in Figure 8-20. You can add an app to a page by using its web address or ID.

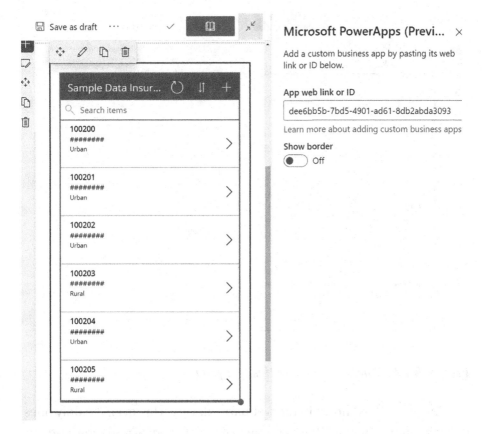

Figure 8-20. *The Power Apps webpart*

Before you start creating a web app, make sure that the site visitors have access to the app before they can see it. Also, you might need to manually test the sizes of the app to make sure that it works properly.

The Page Properties Webpart

The Page Properties webpart is the part of your app that lets you display information about your page, as shown in Figure 8-21 It can also include various other details, such as the title and publisher.

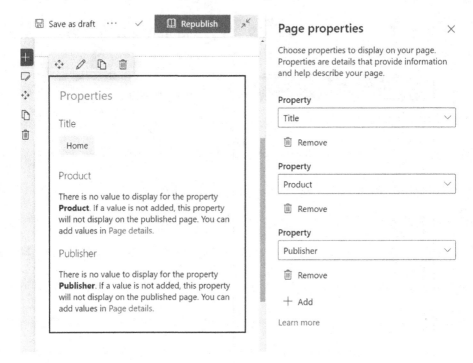

Figure 8-21. *The Page Properties webpart*

The properties shown in the webpart will vary. However, the only ones that it supports are the following: single line of text, date and time, and group managed metadata.

The Markdown Webpart

The Markdown webpart lets you add a type of text known as a markdown to your page. It looks similar to the Code webpart. The right panel shows the most commonly used syntax for this type of text, as shown in Figure 8-22. You can also choose a dark or light theme for this webpart.

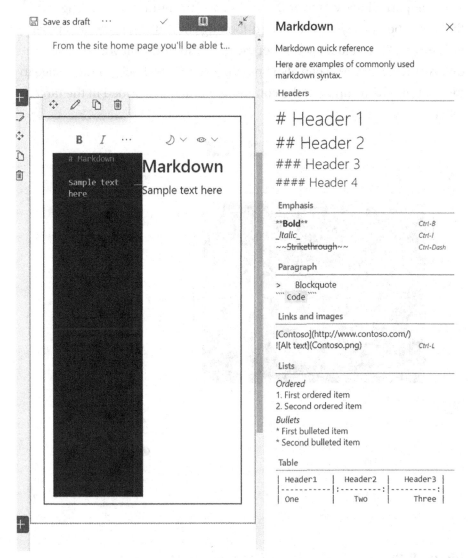

Figure 8-22. *The Markdown webpart*

The Countdown Timer Webpart

This webpart allows you to add a "call to action" button to your page so that it can be displayed with a good-looking countdown timer, as shown in Figure 8-23. You just need to set the date and time that you want to display the button. You can also link the text and the background image to the button. The webpart of the countdown timer is included in the target release program.

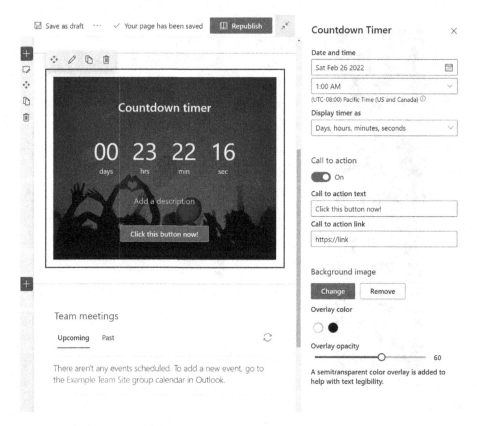

Figure 8-23. *The Countdown Timer webpart*

Summary

You have now come to end of this book and have completed a new journey around SharePoint communication sites. In this age of digital communications, it's critical to create digital experiences for all your users. In this chapter, you learned about digital communication using flow and SharePoint communication sites, about enhanced user collaboration between communication sites and Teams, and finally, about some new webparts of SharePoint communication sites. I hope this journey helps you make digital transformations using communication sites in your organization.

Index

© Charles David Waghmare 2023
C. D. Waghmare, *Beginning SharePoint Communication Sites*,
https://doi.org/10.1007/978-1-4842-8960-0

Printed in the United States
by Baker & Taylor Publisher Services